## Also from the Author

You can develop the skills to meet the needs of learners in any learning environment.

This approachable, in-depth guide unites the adaptability of Universal Design for Learning with the flexibility of blended learning, equipping educators with the tools they need to create relevant, authentic, and meaningful learning pathways to meet students where they're at, no matter the time and place or their pace and path. With step-by-step guidance and clear strategies, authors Katie Novak and Catlin Tucker empower teachers to implement these frameworks in the classroom, with a focus on cultivating community, building equity, and increasing accessibility for all learners.

As we face increasing uncertainty and frequent disruption to traditional ways of living and learning, *UDL and Blended Learning* offers bold, innovative, inclusive solutions for navigating a range of learning landscapes, from the home to the classroom and all points in between, no matter what obstacles may lie ahead.

Catlin Tucker and Katie Novak have worked with too many educators who are frustrated and disillusioned with the teaching profession. They know that teachers are drowning in work and unrealistic demands. Many are mentally and emotionally exhausted by the uncertainty and constant change created by the pandemic. In this follow-up to *UDL and Blended Learning*, the authors have set out to help teachers reimagine their approach to this work so that it is sustainable and rewarding.

Each chapter in *The Shift to Student-Led* takes apart one traditional teacher-led workflow, examining the problems it presents teachers and students, what the research says versus what the reality in the classroom is, and how UDL and blended learning can free teachers from the "sage on the stage" role and place students at the center of their learning. These reimagined student-led workflows help students develop self-awareness, internal motivation, and self-regulation skills, which are critical to becoming expert learners.

Intended for K–12 educators, instructional coaches, and school leaders who want to create academically robust, inclusive learning communities, this book is full of principles, strategies, and resources that can be put into practice right away and at any level.

This book is an essential resource for all educators. To address declining literacy skills, every educator needs to become a teacher of writing. In every grade and subject, the writing process enables students to interpret complex ideas, cultivate their individual voices, and shape and share their learning.

As writing becomes more efficient with the aid of AI chatbots, there's an unparalleled opportunity for educators across all content areas to reimagine their approach to writing. In *Shift Writing into the Classroom*, UDL and blended learning experts Catlin R. Tucker and Katie Novak invite educators to focus on human connection, sitting alongside learners to understand their specific needs and provide individualized instruction and support across *all* grades and content areas. Tucker and Novak transform traditional writing workflows to provide students with meaningful opportunities in the classroom to work through the writing process, collaborate with peers, and produce original writing that addresses task, purpose, and audience creatively and authentically.

Ideal for schools and districts prioritizing the integration of literacy across the curriculum, this book offers practical guidance, strategies, and resources to elevate students' writing abilities in every subject.

Educators understand the crucial importance of developing learning experiences that are accessible, engaging, and student-centered. However, when faced with a long list of ever-increasing demands, teachers are often left without the time, energy, and resources necessary to turn best intentions into best practices. Enter *Elevating Educational Design with AI*, a guide for teachers who want to use technology to activate engagement, give students agency over their learning, and streamline workflows.

In an era when AI is rapidly reshaping our world, some educators feel apprehensive about integrating it into their practice. Without a focus on the humans behind the ideas, AI-generated lessons can end up perpetuating one-size-fits-all learning experiences, undermining efforts to create inclusive and differentiated learning environments where all students can thrive. The conversational, personable, and inquisitive approach of Elevating Educational Design with AI refocuses the conversation on how we can use AI-powered tools in the service of strong pedagogical practices that offer effective learning experiences for every student, demystifying the integration of AI in education, guiding educators, and helping them harness its power.

# Praise for *The Station Rotation Model and UDL*

Catlin Tucker is one of the most brilliant and grounded educators I know. In this book, she brings station rotation and UDL together in a practical and powerful way, because when they're paired—as she says, like peanut butter and jelly—they just work. Her storytelling, examples, and strategies make it all feel SO doable. This is exactly the kind of book teachers need right now and just one more reason Catlin remains the QUEEN of blended learning.

> —**Katie Novak, Ed.D.,** internationally recognized UDL expert and author of sixteen books, including four co-authored with Dr. Catlin Tucker

Dr. Catlin Tucker's *The Station Rotation Model* is a transformative guide for educators seeking to elevate Tier 1 instruction and empower every learner. Grounded in Universal Design for Learning and MTSS, it offers a clear, practical blueprint for designing inclusive, student-centered classrooms that prioritize differentiation, engagement, and agency. With actionable strategies and a mindset shift toward flexibility, this book helps educators create learning environments that meet diverse needs while building critical competencies. It's a must-read for anyone committed to making learning more personalized, equitable, and impactful.

> —**Eric Sheninger,** bestselling author and speaker

Dr. Catlin Tucker's latest work is an inspiring and practical guide for educators seeking to move beyond the traditional one-size-fits-all model. Through real-world stories, a data-driven approach to design, and a clear implementation path for the Station Rotation Model, Tucker shows how to make differentiation realistic and sustainable. I wholeheartedly support, use, and believe in the strategies she shares, particularly her strong case for moving away from only using whole-group instruction to meet the diverse needs of all learners and integrating a model that supports small-group instruction. Her focus on purposeful technology integration, UDL, and blended learning applies across all grade levels, K–12, making this model impactful everywhere. The built-in reflection, discussion points, and "Your Turn" sections turn this quick read into a powerful resource that every educator can immediately put into practice.

—**Nicki Slaugh,** principal, author, and speaker

Station rotation is a powerful, evidence-based model for meeting diverse learners' needs. This practical, engaging, and inspiring book can help any teacher, in any subject area or school, implement actionable strategies that keep learners engaged and make teaching fun. I hope my kids' teachers will read this book —and I plan to get them copies!

—**Robert Barnett,** co-founder of Modern Classrooms Project and author of *Meet Every Learner's Needs*

Dr. Tucker states it best when she points out the fact that "we talk a lot about the importance of equity in education, but teachers who use one-size-fits-all lessons are, at best, providing only an equal experience." Our educators have a lot on their plates, and with how diverse our students are, it can be challenging to find ways to support all students. Recognizing this, Dr. Tucker's book dives into how implementing the Station Rotation Model, with the foundations of Universal Design for Learning and Multi-Tier Systems of Support, can help elevate Tier 1 instruction and empower students to become their own active agents in their learning journey, allowing educators to truly differentiate instruction to meet the needs of their students.

As someone who works with educators daily, looking to differentiate instruction and meet the needs of their students, I highly recommend this book. It contains actionable steps that any educator, novice to veteran, can take and implement the next day.

—**Christopher Hoang, Ed.D.,** assistant director, Technology Innovation and Outreach at the Los Angeles County Office of Education

Too often, UDL and MTSS live in theory without a bridge to classroom practice. Dr. Tucker builds that bridge. This book gives educators the tools to differentiate meaningfully, design with learner variability in mind, and create proactive structures that reduce barriers before they arise. It's both a mindset shift and a practical road map. This book couldn't be more timely or relevant!

 **—Robert Mayfield,** high school educator, instructional coach, and college instructor

I've been in over a thousand classrooms in six states and four countries since 2022. Everywhere I go, people are trying small groups. But the implementation is not being done well. When I share Dr. Tucker's techniques, classrooms light up with station rotation. I'm excited for this book so that more classrooms can come on board!

 **—Jon Corippo,** global educator, pedagogist, and author

# The Station Rotation Model and UDL

# THE STATION ROTATION MODEL & UDL

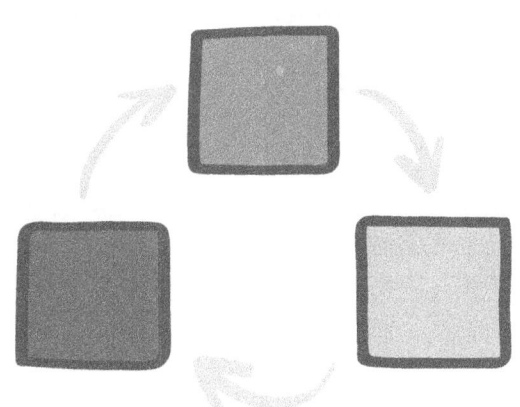

**Elevate Tier 1 Instruction**
and Cultivate Learner Agency

Catlin R. Tucker

*The Station Rotation Model and UDL: Elevate Tier 1 Instruction and Cultivate Learner Agency*
© 2025 Catlin R. Tucker

All rights reserved. No part of this publication may be reproduced in any form or by any electronic or mechanical means, including information storage and retrieval systems, without permission in writing by the publisher, except by a reviewer who may quote brief passages in a review. For information regarding permission, contact the publisher at books@impressbooks.org.

> This book is available at special discounts when purchased in quantity for educational purposes or for use as premiums, promotions, or fundraisers. For inquiries and details, contact the publisher at books@impressbooks.org.

Published by IMPress, a division of Dave Burgess Consulting, Inc.
IMPressbooks.org
DaveBurgessConsulting.com
San Diego, CA

Library of Congress Control Number: 2025938431
Paperback ISBN: 978-1-948334-81-5
Ebook ISBN: 978-1-948334-82-2

Cover and interior design by Liz Schreiter
Edited and produced by Reading List Editorial
ReadingListEditorial.com

For every educator daring to do things differently.

And for every student, who deserves to be seen, heard, and supported.

This work is for you.

# Contents

**Introduction** .................................................... 1

## PART I: WHY THE STATION ROTATION MODEL?

**Chapter 1:** UDL and Blended Learning: The Ultimate Power Couple .................................................... 10

**Chapter 2:** Understanding the Station Rotation Model .......... 29

**Chapter 3:** Elevating Tier 1 Instruction with the Station Rotation Model .................................................... 55

## PART II: IMPLEMENTING THE STATION ROTATION MODEL

**Chapter 4:** Data-Informed Design ........................... 74

**Chapter 5:** Assessment ..................................... 82

**Chapter 6:** The Teacher-Led Station and Differentiation ........ 109

**Chapter 7:** The Online Station and the Four Cs of Twenty-First-Century Learning ............................... 149

**Chapter 8:** The Offline Station and Student Agency ........... 168

## PART III: INNOVATING THE STATION ROTATION MODEL

**Chapter 9:** Supporting Executive Functioning with Station Rotation 198

**Chapter 10:** Logistics and Setting the Stage for Station Rotation Success .................................................... 215

**Chapter 11:** Creative Alternatives to the Traditional Station Rotation .................................................... 237

**Conclusion** .................................................... 252

References .................................................... 255
Acknowledgments ............................................... 258
About Catlin R. Tucker ......................................... 259
More from IMPress ............................................. 261

# Tables, Figures, and Planning Templates

Table 1.1: UDL Principles Explained .......................... 15

Figure 1.1: The Shift from Whole-Group to Small-Group Instruction with Blended Learning ........................................ 20

Figure 2.1: The Basic Design of the Station Rotation Model ....... 31

Table 2.1: Station Types and Their Instructional Purpose ......... 32

Table 2.2: Classic Learning Centers vs. the Station Rotation Model ...................................................... 36

Table 2.3: High School Biology Lesson—Basic vs. Intentional Design ..................................................... 39

Figure 2.2: Linear Lesson Reimagined with the Station Rotation Model ...................................................... 42

Figure 3.1: Multi-Tiered System of Supports ..................... 61

Figure 4.1: Data-Informed Design Cycle ......................... 78

Table 5.1: Pre-Assessment Strategies ........................... 85

Table 5.2: Middle School Science Example: Standards-Aligned Pre-Assessment ............................................... 86

Table 5.3: Elementary Math Example: Standards-Aligned Pre-Assessment ............................................... 88

Table 5.4: Differentiate Entry Points Based on Pre-Assessment Data ....................................................... 90

Table 5.5: Four-Point Asset-Based Reciprocal Teaching Rubric .... 95

Table 5.6: Formative Assessment Strategies ..................... 96

Table 5.7: Elementary Example: English Language Arts (ELA) ...... 98

Table 5.8: Secondary Example: Social Studies ................... 99

Table 5.9: Elementary Summative Assessment Example: Math ... 101

Table 5.10: Secondary Summative Assessment Example: English .................................................... 102

Table 5.11: Elementary Math Assessment: Standards-Aligned, Asset-Based Rubric .................................... 103

Table 5.12: Secondary English Assessment: Standards-Aligned, Asset-Based Rubric .................................... 104

Table 6.1: Classroom Elements to Differentiate Paired with Examples ................................................. 114

Table 6.2: Skill-Level vs. Mixed-Skill-Level Groupings at the Teacher-Led Station ........................................ 119

Table 6.3: Differentiating "I Do, We Do, Pairs Do, You Do" ....... 122

Table 6.4: Differentiating Hook the Group ..................... 127

Table 6.5: Differentiating the Concept Attainment Model ........ 132

Table 6.6: Differentiating Real-Time Formative Feedback ........ 137

Table 6.7: Differentiating Present-Pause-Discuss-Adjust ........ 142

Table 7.1: The Four Cs ...................................... 153

Table 7.2: Understanding the Four Cs ......................... 156

Table 7.3: Providing Multiple Means at the Online Station ....... 161

Table 7.4: The SAMR Framework ............................. 163

Figure 8.1: Three Psychological Needs Required for Motivation .. 171

Table 8.1: "Would You Rather" Options ....................... 175

Table 8.2: Providing Multiple Means at the Offline Station ...... 177

Table 8.3: Meaning-Making Activities: "Would You Rather" Options ................................................... 180

Figure 8.2: Goal-Setting Graphic Organizer ................... 183

Figure 8.3: Pre-Planning Document .......................... 185

Figure 8.4: See, Think, Wonder Thinking Routine .............. 186

Figure 8.5: Connect, Extend, Challenge Thinking Routine ....... 188

Figure 8.6: Emoji Hands Self-Assessment Document ........... 191

Figure 8.7: 3-2-1 Reflection ................................. 192

Table 9.1: Executive Functioning and the Station Rotation Model ................................................... 201

Figure 9.1: Elementary Relaxation Station Mini-Playlist ......... 203

Figure 9.2: Secondary Relaxation Station Mini-Playlist .......... 204

Table 9.2: Co-Creating Class Norms .......................... 208

Table 9.3: Path of Consequences for Behaviors That Violate Class Agreements ................................................ 210

Table 9.4: Safe Space Reflection Form ........................ 211

Table 10.1: Grouping Strategies .............................. 218

Figure 10.1: Station Rotation Grouping Display ................ 220

Table 10.2: Types of Engagement and the Furniture Arrangements That Work Best ............................................. 222

Figure 10.2: U-Shaped Teacher-Led Station .................... 223

Figure 10.3: Rows for Independent Work ...................... 224

Figure 10.4: Table Groups for Collaborative Tasks or Discussion ................................................. 225

Table 10.3: The Components of a Seamless Transition .......... 227

Table 10.4: Strategies for Fast Finishers ...................... 229

Figure 10.5: Brain Break Choice Board ........................ 230

Table 10.5: Station Rotation Lesson Checklist ................. 231

Table 11.1: Learning Activities That Benefit from Self-Pacing ..... 241

Figure 11.1: Must-Do vs. May-Do Station Rotation Personalized Learning Plan .............................................. 244

# Introduction

In today's classrooms, educators are working with students who bring a wide range of strengths, needs, interests, and experiences to the learning environment. While this diversity enriches classroom communities, it also requires instructional models that are flexible, inclusive, and responsive. Traditional, one-size-fits-all teaching methods fall short in addressing the dynamic needs of diverse learners, leaving many students disengaged and underserved, while many teachers are frustrated and burned out.

Thankfully, lots of teachers have embraced the opportunity to reimagine what teaching and learning looks like, adopting differentiated approaches to instruction and more student-centered pedagogies.[1] Two trends that exemplify this shift are the growing emphasis on Universal Design for Learning (UDL), a proactive framework that strives to make learning accessible, inclusive, and equitable to meet the needs of all learners. At the same time, the integration of technology in education has paved the way for innovative, technology-enhanced instructional models that can make accomplishing the goals of UDL more manageable.[2] Among these technology-enhanced instructional strategies, the Station Rotation Model presents a clear path to accommodating learner variability in the classroom while also fostering a more engaging and effective learning environment for all.

## The Station Rotation Model and UDL

This book is dedicated to exploring the Station Rotation Model in depth, offering practical insights and strategies for teachers who are committed to transforming their classrooms and enhancing student learning. I want to empower educators to create learning experiences that are more equitable and sustainable by giving students more control over the pace, path, and process of their learning. Ultimately, I hope that readers will feel empowered to design instruction that meets students where they are—and that students, in turn, will feel more seen, supported, and successful.

## Why Did I Write This Book?

Recognizing and honoring each student's unique qualities, identities, and backgrounds is essential for cultivating an inclusive and effective learning environment. In my twenty-four years as an educator, I've witnessed the spectrum of needs in classrooms expand significantly every year. Unfortunately, when the only instructional model at teachers' disposal is the whole-group, teacher-led, and teacher-paced lesson, this increasing diversity is often perceived as problematic or a threat to learning. However, the diversity of skills, abilities, needs, language proficiencies, and learning preferences in our classrooms is not a threat or a problem; it is a reality we must design for. Designing for learner variability and tailoring our approaches to meet the diverse needs of our students has the added benefit of transforming this diversity into a valuable asset.

> *The diversity of skills, abilities, needs, language proficiencies, and learning preferences in our classrooms is not a threat or a problem; it is a reality we must design for.*

# Introduction

We talk a lot about the importance of equity in education, but teachers who use the one-size-fits-all lesson are, at best, providing only an *equal* experience. Equality is not the same as equity. Equity acknowledges that individual students need individual inputs (e.g., teacher time and energy, scaffolding, feedback) to reach a particular output, or learning objective. But how do we provide those individual inputs needed to honor learner variability when we are trapped at the front of the room, transferring information and orchestrating the parts of a whole-group lesson?

I've written a collection of books about blended learning over the last fifteen years; however, the Station Rotation Model continues to be a favorite technology-enhanced instructional model when schools and districts hire me and my team to work with their teachers on the shift from whole-group, teacher-led, teacher-paced instruction to small-group, differentiated instruction and student-led learning. The Station Rotation Model can remove barriers, provide flexible learning pathways, and enable students to make meaning on their own and with their peers. Unlike a traditional whole-group lesson, the Station Rotation Model provides students with more control over the pace and the path of their learning. As students move through a rotation where they engage in individual and collaborative tasks independent of the teacher, they develop essential self-regulation skills that foster independence, confidence, and a greater sense of ownership over their learning.

The Station Rotation Model is a blended learning model that rotates students through a series of stations, or learning activities. The rotation is composed of three types of stations: a teacher-led, online, and offline station. When implemented thoughtfully, station rotation balances strategic technology use with meaningful offline learning experiences, ensuring students engage in diverse, dynamic, and interactive learning opportunities.

The Station Rotation Model is a K–12 instructional approach that creates dedicated time for teachers to work with small groups of students, meeting their specific needs. This level of direct, differentiated engagement is impossible to achieve in a whole-group lesson where teachers present the same information in the same way for all students. Instead of giving all students in a class the same experience and access to resources, the Station Rotation Model presents a sustainable path toward designing lessons that strive to meet each student's needs, providing an equitable learning experience.

In the last five years, my work on blended learning has intersected with Dr. Katie Novak's work on UDL, which we will explore in the next chapter. I've had the pleasure of authoring four books with Katie about the synergy between blended learning and UDL. In those books, our goal was to help educators use blended learning models to make implementing UDL more manageable and sustainable. The goal of *this* work is to ensure learning is accessible, inclusive, and equitable. That is why I have anchored this book in UDL: I want educators to feel confident they can implement the core principles of equitable pedagogy in their classrooms consistently and effectively.

## How to Use This Book

The goal of this book is to help educators understand how they can put the principles and guidelines at the heart of UDL into practice using the Station Rotation Model. Broadly, then, this book has two aims: 1) to introduce the principles of UDL and blended learning and 2) to explain the on-the-ground process of putting the principles at the heart of UDL into practice with the Station Rotation Model. I discuss the latter specifically so that readers can successfully and sustainably design lessons that meet the needs of diverse groups of students. With an emphasis on practical application, the bulk of the book will guide you through the process of designing high-level, data-informed station rotation lessons that prioritize differentiation and student agency to elevate the teaching and learning experience for everyone!

Part I of this project ("Why the Station Rotation Model?") focuses on explaining the theoretical foundations for UDL, blended learning, and the Station Rotation Model. However, my ultimate aspiration here is to transform pedagogical practice. Toward that end, part II of this book ("Implementing the Station Rotation Model") will help readers bring UDL and blended learning to fruition through a series of impactful and iterative best practices with the Station Rotation Model. The cornerstone of part II, then, is the Data-Informed Design Cycle, a step-by-step model that guides readers to adopt and implement the Station Rotation Model in ways that meet the shifting, specific needs of their students. By emphasizing a data-driven approach to design, this book offers a pathway toward intentional implementation of the Station Rotation Model. Each step of that design process is unpacked in detail over the course of the chapters in part II and explored as an opportunity to embrace the central ideals of UDL. Following that blueprint for success, part III ("Innovating the Station Rotation Model") challenges readers to approach the Station Rotation Model as a flexible pedagogical practice that they can—and should—reinvent with the ever-expanding needs of their students in mind.

The activities and examples throughout this text are designed for adaptability and approachability. However, my hope is to empower readers to embrace UDL fully and implement it thoughtfully, rather than simply to offer plug-and-play, one-size-fits-all activities. Such an automatic, generic approach to the Station Rotation Model would, after all, run contrary to the spirit of UDL and would likely fail to address the needs, abilities, interests, preferences, and aspirations of each reader's individual students.

For readability and ease of reference, chapters in this book follow a regular sequence:

1. Each chapter begins with a story or *anecdote*. These stories make clear connections between the main ideas in the chapter and real-world experiences to ground this new learning in relatable stories.
2. Following the opening story, I take an outcomes-oriented approach by listing *firm goals* for each chapter. I want to model the importance of articulating firm goals so learners (in this case, you!) know what we are working toward.
3. Throughout each chapter, I provide *explanations and examples* to help you understand key concepts so that you can implement specific strategies. My examples span kindergarten through twelfth grade to demonstrate that educators at any grade level can use the Station Rotation Model to enhance and improve the quality of learning. That breadth also underscores that all educators can employ UDL principles to more effectively design for learner variability in their classrooms.
4. At the end of each chapter, I provide a short *summary*.
5. Next, I offer a section for you to *reflect and discuss* with prompts and questions. I encourage you to engage with this material in the way that best suits your learning preferences and allows you to think deeply and meaningfully about the content. For example, you could choose personal reflection (e.g., writing, drawing, audio recordings, or social media posts), or you could have an in-person or asynchronous online discussion with colleagues.
6. Finally, it's *time to apply* what you've read with an activity that encourages you to take what you're learning and act on it immediately.

# Introduction

This book is designed to meet the needs of four major groups of readers: new teachers, seasoned educators, instructional coaches, and K–12 administrators.

Additionally, this book equips future teachers with the knowledge and skills to effectively design and implement differentiated small-group instruction. By learning to create universally designed lessons, educators can provide students with opportunities to develop as self-directed learners capable of navigating their learning journeys. This preparation ensures that new teachers enter the profession ready to meet the diverse needs in their classrooms.

For any experienced educator frustrated by the lackluster results of one-size-fits-all lessons, this book offers a comprehensive, user-friendly guide to universally designing lessons. By adopting the Station Rotation Model, teachers can create more engaging, personalized learning experiences that cater to their students' diverse needs.[3]

By fostering a culture of personalized learning, school leaders can drive systemic change that promotes equity and excellence across their institutions. This book is a valuable resource for school leaders, administrators, and instructional coaches working to support teachers in shifting instructional practices. It provides a clear framework for implementing the Station Rotation Model, helping educators meet their students' academic and social-emotional learning needs.

As we embark on this journey together, remember that the Station Rotation Model is more than just a technology-enhanced instructional model; it is a mindset shift toward creating more inclusive, engaging, and effective learning environments. By embracing this model, you are taking a significant step toward honoring the unique needs and qualities of each student and fostering a classroom culture that values and leverages diversity. I hope this book inspires you to explore new ways to elevate your teaching and make a lasting impact on your students' lives.

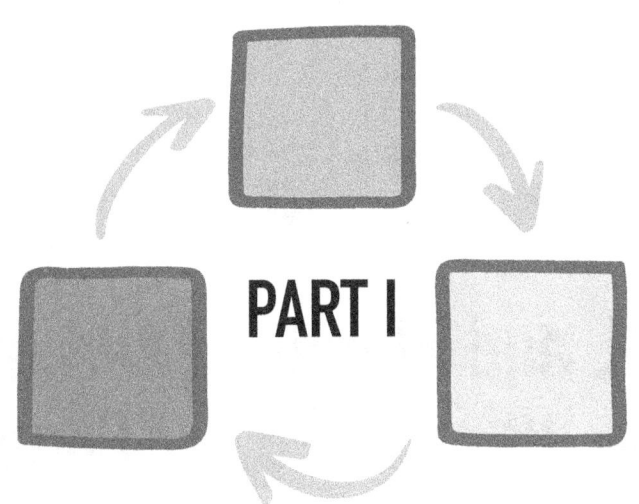

# WHY THE STATION ROTATION MODEL?

**CHAPTER 1**

# UDL and Blended Learning: The Ultimate Power Couple

## A Game Changer: How Station Rotation Transformed My Teaching

Five years into my teaching career, I hit a wall. I remember sitting in my classroom after school one day, exhausted, thinking: *Have I made an enormous mistake coming into this profession?*

I had entered education with a vision of students bounding through the door, eager to learn and engage in deep, meaningful discussions. Instead, most of the teenagers in my high school English class sat slumped in their chairs uninterested and disengaged. I felt like I was failing—not just failing my students but failing to create the dynamic learning environment I had dreamed of while working on my English credential and masters in education.

By 2007, I was at a crossroads. I gave myself one more year to turn things around, or I'd walk away from teaching entirely. I began treating my classroom like a lab, experimenting and embracing any strategy that might engage my students. I was especially curious about leveraging the devices a handful of my students carried in their pockets. Their phones offered a chance to connect them with resources beyond our classroom walls (without requiring a class set of computers). I started searching for ways to design lessons that used these limited devices meaningfully. That search led me to the Station Rotation Model. Everything changed.

At its core, the Station Rotation Model allowed me to meet the diverse needs of my students in ways that whole-group, teacher-led instruction never could. I had second-language learners who needed structured support with reading and writing, students with individualized education plans (IEPs) and 504 plans who needed specific accommodations, and a classroom full of kids at different skill levels, learning preferences, and interests. Instead of trying to squeeze in additional support during breaks or after school, I could work with students in small groups, offering tailored instruction during our actual class.

Beyond differentiation, the energy in my classroom shifted. At the online station, students weren't passively consuming content—they were collaborating. Huddled around shared devices, they engaged in discussion, analyzed texts together, and offered one another feedback. The offline stations gave students more control over the pace of their work and the freedom to make decisions about how they approached tasks. They had opportunities to choose pathways, revisit materials, and explore concepts in ways that made sense to *them*. Learning was no longer something they simply received; it was something they actively engaged in.

What I hadn't realized at the time was that I was naturally merging Universal Design for Learning (UDL) and blended learning. The Station Rotation Model made it possible to move beyond a one-size-fits-all approach to offer multiple means of engagement, representation, and action and expression, ensuring students had different ways to access information, interact with content, make meaning, and demonstrate understanding. It wasn't just about using technology—it was about removing barriers to learning and honoring student agency.

Simply put, shifting to blended learning and the Station Rotation Model saved my career. It allowed me to design for the diverse needs of my students, give them more control over their learning, and create a classroom that felt more dynamic, inclusive, and student centered.

UDL, with its goal of supporting learner agency and making learning accessible for all students, can sometimes feel challenging to put into practice without the right tools and strategies. It's a framework that promises to positively impact students, but educators often struggle with the "how" of implementing it effectively. Like peanut butter without jelly, UDL can be dense and hard to work with, its principles getting "stuck" without the practical methods to put them into practice smoothly.

This is where blended learning comes in. By integrating technology strategically to free teachers from the front of the room, blended learning, generally, and the Station Rotation Model, specifically, provide the practical means to realize UDL's goals. This approach offers flexibility and personalization that can adapt to diverse learner needs, making those lofty aims achievable.

Conversely, blended learning without UDL can lead to shallow technology integration. It's easy to get caught up in the bells and whistles of new technology tools without considering their true educational value. Without the guiding principles of UDL, the Station Rotation Model can become a collection of disconnected activities that lack a higher purpose. Like jelly without peanut butter, it can be sweet but insubstantial, missing the strong pedagogical practices needed to make a real impact. UDL gives the Station Rotation Model direction and depth, ensuring that technology serves to enhance learning experiences and meet the needs of *all* students.

Just like the perfect balance of peanut butter and jelly, UDL and station rotation together create a powerful synergy. They complement each other, each bringing out the best in the other, making teaching and learning both more effective and more enjoyable.

# Firm Goals

By the end of this chapter, you will:

- Gain a comprehensive understanding of UDL and its core beliefs and learn how UDL supports inclusive, accessible, and equitable learning environments.
- Be able to define, explain, and understand how blended learning (generally) and the Station Rotation Model (specifically) shift classroom dynamics from teacher centered to student centered, fostering learner agency and providing flexible learning pathways.
- Understand how UDL and station rotation complement one another, creating a practical, flexible approach to designing and facilitating learning experiences that meet the needs of all students.

# UDL Guidelines

UDL is a framework that acknowledges and embraces the diverse ways students engage with and process information. Rooted in neuroscience and educational research, UDL shifts away from a one-size-fits-all approach and instead encourages educators to proactively design learning experiences that anticipate variability. A UDL-driven classroom looks and feels different from the traditional teacher-led, direct instruction model. It is a proactive approach that ensures all students—regardless of background, ability, or learning preferences—have equitable access to rigorous, meaningful learning experiences from the outset. This is a far better approach than reacting to challenges by modifying instruction after the fact.

For example, a history lesson on the Civil Rights Movement might include a combination of primary source videos, podcasts, and text-based materials so students can engage with content in ways that best suit their needs. In a science classroom, students may demonstrate their understanding of a concept by creating a visual model, recording a video explanation, or engaging in a hands-on experiment. In writing instruction, a teacher might offer students digital annotation tools, voice-to-text software, or guided graphic organizers to support their thinking. At its core, UDL strives to remove barriers and foster engagement and agency, ensuring students have the tools and opportunities to learn in ways that work best for them *before* challenges arise.

The UDL Guidelines developed by CAST (Center for Applied Special Technology) are organized around three core principles—engagement, representation, and action and expression—which help ensure that learning is accessible, meaningful, and effective for every student.[1] Let's explore each principle in depth and consider examples of how they can be applied in the classroom, as pictured in table 1.1.

### Table 1.1: UDL Principles Explained

| Principle | What Is It? | What Does It Look Like in Action? |
|---|---|---|
| **Multiple means of engagement** | This offers students different ways to connect with learning by tapping into their interests, motivations, and preferences. Since students bring diverse identities, experiences, and needs, there is no single pathway that will engage all students. Thus, providing various options ensures that all learners can make meaningful connections to course content. | Would you rather explore a new concept through a hands-on activity with materials or dive into a video or article that explains the concept?<br><br>Would you rather participate in a class discussion where you share your ideas in real time or reflect privately in a journal before sharing with your peers?<br><br>Would you rather work independently on a project and set your own timeline or collaborate with a small group where everyone contributes ideas and determines the scope and timeline? |
| **Multiple means of representation** | This offers learners different ways to access and interpret information. Because students have diverse backgrounds, abilities, and learning preferences, providing a variety of ways to represent content—visual, auditory, textual, or interactive formats—ensures that all learners can perceive, understand, and make meaning of the material. | Would you rather watch a video with visual explanations or listen to an audio recording or podcast?<br><br>Would you rather experience a live demonstration of a process or read a step-by-step explanation of how to do it?<br><br>Would you rather get information from explicit instruction provided by the teacher or explore the concept on your own using written materials and examples? |

| Multiple means of action and expression | This offers learners different ways to interact with learning materials and demonstrate what they know. Since learners vary in how they navigate tasks and express their understanding, offering options—such as writing, speaking, creating visual projects, or using technology—ensures that all students can showcase their knowledge in ways that align with their strengths and preferences. These options also allow learners to develop strategic skills like planning, organization, and self-regulation. | Would you rather write an essay to explain what you've learned or create a video presentation that demonstrates your understanding?<br><br>Would you rather complete a digital project using multimedia tools or express your knowledge through a hands-on demonstration or physical project?<br><br>Would you rather respond to a prompt using speech-to-text technology or type out your thoughts in a written format? |
|---|---|---|

The UDL Guidelines emphasize that each learner is unique. This variability influences students' motivations, their perception and processing of information, and the ways they demonstrate understanding. To effectively honor our students' variability, we must design lessons that acknowledge and take these differences into account by offering students multiple pathways to engage with content, make meaning, and express their knowledge. By doing so, we create learning environments that attempt to meet individual needs and preferences, empowering students to take ownership of their learning.

CAST emphasizes that the principles and guidelines are meant to develop and evolve over time. In July 2024, CAST released version 3.0 of their framework, which is the fifth iteration of the guidelines and is designed to keep up with research and practitioner feedback. UDL has always focused on creating learning environments that strive to ensure all students can make progress toward learning goals and objectives. The latest version of the guidelines takes this further by connecting UDL to asset-based pedagogies or specific teaching methods that focus on a student's strengths and potential. The purpose is to show how UDL aligns with these approaches and how every student brings their unique skills and backgrounds to the learning process.

## UDL Core Beliefs

At the heart of UDL are several foundational beliefs that guide its implementation and ensure its effectiveness in diverse learning environments. Understanding these core beliefs is essential for educators to design and facilitate truly inclusive and equitable learning experiences. Keep these key ideas in mind:

- **Variability is the norm, not the exception:** Every learner is unique, bringing different strengths, needs, learning preferences, interests, and identities to the learning environment. UDL recognizes and celebrates this variability, designing flexible learning experiences to meet learners' diverse needs.
- **Learning is multidimensional:** Effective learning involves multiple brain networks—affective (the why), recognition (the what), and strategic (the how). UDL addresses these different dimensions to support comprehensive learning.
- **Accessibility is for all:** UDL strives to remove barriers to learning, ensuring that all students, regardless of their background or ability, have equal opportunities to succeed. This is grounded in the belief that all students can reach firm, standards-aligned goals when they are provided with flexible pathways through the learning experience.

These core beliefs represent a fundamental shift in how educators approach teaching and learning. Rather than expecting students to conform to rigid instructional methods, UDL challenges educators to design learning environments that embrace variability from the start. This shift is revolutionary because it moves away from outdated, deficit-based thinking, which often views differences as obstacles to overcome, and instead positions diversity as a strength. By acknowledging that learning is multidimensional and shaped by affective, recognition, and strategic networks, UDL ensures that instruction is more engaging and responsive to students' needs.

At its core, UDL was developed to address systemic barriers that have historically excluded or marginalized students, especially those with disabilities, multilingual learners, and students from diverse cultural and socioeconomic backgrounds. Instead of offering one-size-fits-all instruction and retrofitting accommodations when students struggle, UDL provides proactive, flexible pathways that empower all learners to reach high expectations in ways that honor their strengths and needs. This represents a critical reimagining of what equitable education should look like—an environment where accessibility, engagement, and student agency are not afterthoughts but integrated into the fabric of instructional design.

# Blended Learning

Blended learning combines active, engaged learning online and active, engaged learning offline to give students more control over the time, place, pace, and path of their learning.

It is not simply about using technology—it is about leveraging digital tools strategically to enhance personalization, differentiation, and accessibility in learning experiences. Effective blended learning environments provide multiple pathways for students to engage with content, collaborate with peers, and demonstrate their understanding, ensuring that learning is both flexible and student centered. At its best, blended learning shifts the teacher's role from content deliverer to facilitator, allowing for more meaningful interactions, targeted small-group instruction, and deeper student engagement.

*Blended learning* is a phrase many educators were not familiar with before the COVID-19 pandemic. Their introduction to this phrase was during one of the most challenging moments in their careers, when they had to shift from in-person to online teaching without any preparation or training. It's not surprising, then, that many teachers have misconceptions, or even negative feelings, about blended learning.

---

*Blended learning combines active, engaged learning online and active, engaged learning offline to give students more control over the time, place, pace, and path of their learning.*

---

Blended learning's combination of online and offline learning can take many forms. It can happen entirely in a classroom, using strategies such as the Station Rotation Model, and it can extend beyond the classroom, with more emphasis on the online learning element. In this book, we will focus specifically on the Station Rotation Model as a way to put the core beliefs of UDL into practice in a practical and consistent way.

## Shifting the Focus to Learners with Blended Learning

The goal of blended learning and the Station Rotation Model is to shift control over learning from teacher to student. Students won't control time, place, pace, and path all of the time, but blended learning's combination of online and offline learning is designed to give them *more* control, *more* of the time. Releasing control and trusting our students to share the responsibility for learning is central to blended learning and is reflected in the new version of the UDL Guidelines. Trust is also necessary if we hope to help students cultivate the skills and confidence needed to navigate a rapidly changing world.

Blended learning strives to position students at the center of the learning experience and free teachers from the front of the room, as pictured in figure 1.1. Instead of dedicating significant portions of class to the transfer of information, teachers are free to engage in high-impact instructional strategies.

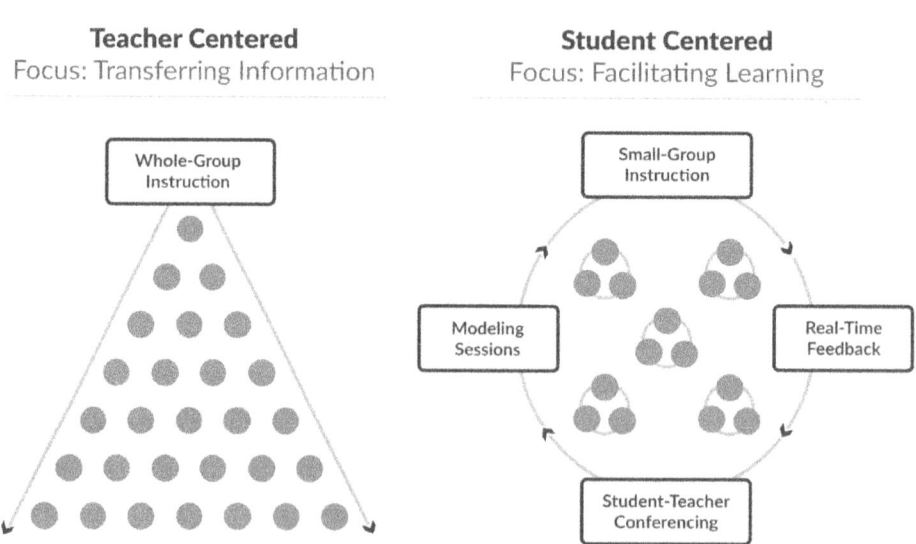

**Figure 1.1: The Shift from Whole-Group to Small-Group Instruction with Blended Learning**

If we are truly committed to designing learning experiences that meet each student where they are, blended learning provides a more sustainable way to achieve this goal. By shifting away from the traditional whole-group, teacher-led model of instruction, educators can focus their time and energy on high-impact strategies that address individual student needs. Teachers have the time and space to facilitate differentiated small-group instruction, lead modeling sessions that target different learning levels, provide timely and actionable feedback as students work, and conference with learners to track their progress and better understand their needs.

Blended learning moves us from a model focused on equality, where every student receives the same instruction and access to your time and energy, to one that promotes equity, ensuring every student gets the support they need to succeed. This aligns perfectly with the UDL framework, which emphasizes flexibility, learner agency, and personalized learning paths. By leveraging blended learning approaches such as the Station Rotation Model, teachers can create more equitable, personalized learning experiences that foster growth in all students.

## UDL and Blended Learning

When Dr. Katie Novak and I wrote our first book together, *UDL and Blended Learning*, our goal was to help educators understand how combining these two powerful frameworks could make them both more effective. We recognized that while UDL provides the foundation for creating inclusive, equitable learning environments, blended learning models offer practical strategies that allow teachers to create flexible pathways, putting UDL into practice. Without the structure of blended learning, implementing UDL can feel overwhelming for educators trying to meet the diverse needs of every learner. Conversely, without the guiding principles of UDL, blended learning can risk becoming shallow, focused more on technology use than on achieving meaningful, student-centered learning.

# UDL and Blended Learning in Action: A Fifth-Grade Math Classroom

When I began coaching a fifth-grade teacher who was feeling overwhelmed by the diverse needs in her math class, I immediately recognized a common challenge. Her mini-lessons—meant to last twenty minutes—were consistently stretching into forty-minute marathons. A handful of students needed more scaffolded instruction and support, while the rest of the class sat bored, waiting, and disengaged. Despite the lackluster results of this whole-group approach to instruction, she was initially resistant to change. She wanted to see the Station Rotation Model in action and asked me to design and facilitate a lesson for her students.

I designed a four-station rotation, and the scenes that unfolded at each station were the best endorsement I could give for the value of the Station Rotation Model in providing students with multiple ways to engage with math content.

At station 1, students worked online with Desmos, playing a game that challenged them to identify a mystery shape by asking strategic yes-or-no questions. Paired up and using laptops, learners leaned in, eyes darting across the grid of quadrilaterals as they eliminated possibilities one by one. "Does your shape have four equal sides?" one student asked, prompting their partner's nod and a flurry of clicks. The activity transformed vocabulary practice into a game of logic and deduction. Students spoke confidently about parallel lines, right angles, and congruent sides, often pausing midgame to jot down new terms. Engagement buzzed at a low hum—thoughtful, focused, and full of collaborative energy. For learners who needed language support or a confidence boost, sentence stems and a visual glossary were available at their desks to support their participation.

At station 2, students worked in pairs to play Always, Sometimes, Never, a discussion-based challenge that required them to consider and defend claims about geometric properties. With handouts and colored pencils, students debated each statement: "A square is a rhombus," "A triangle is a parallelogram," "A trapezoid is a quadrilateral." As they agreed or disagreed, they drew quick sketches to prove their thinking, pointing out side lengths, angles, and other visual evidence. "This is sometimes true—look, here's why!" one student exclaimed, holding up a drawing to support their claim. The back-and-forth was rich and animated, with students engaging in mathematical discourse that deepened their understanding through peer conversation and visual reasoning. For those who needed a challenge, optional extension statements pushed their thinking. Students engaged in collaborative dialogue, using language, visuals, and multiple representations to support their conclusions.

At station 3, students grabbed whiteboards, protractors, and colorful markers to play Fun with Angles, a partner game that challenged them to measure and check each other's work. Each board featured three pieces of tape crisscrossing at random angles, setting the stage for a hands-on angle-measurement challenge. After measuring one of the angles and writing the degree, students traded boards and checked their partner's accuracy. Correct answers stayed; mistakes were erased and rewritten in a different color. "You were off by five degrees—I got forty-seven," one student said with a smile, marking it in blue next to the erased black number. The friendly competition sparked laughter and concentration in equal measure, giving students meaningful practice in a low-stakes, high-engagement format. For students needing additional support, angle reference cards and labeled protractors were available.

At the teacher-led station, students gathered at a small table for a game of Mystery Shape Investigation—a hook designed to introduce the next concept in their geometry unit. Although the group was of mixed ability, I intentionally paired students with similar readiness levels and gave each pair a sealed envelope containing a clue card tailored to what they could access. "This shape has four sides. Two sides are parallel. One angle is greater than ninety degrees, and one is less," one pair read aloud. Immediately, whiteboards came out as students made predictions and sketched possibilities. Some drew confidently, while others asked questions or hesitated, trying to recall the properties of parallelograms or trapezoids. As pairs worked through their clues, I facilitated with guiding questions like "What do you know about opposite angles in this shape?" or "Could more than one shape fit this clue?" Pairs with stronger skills tackled more complex clues involving multiple constraints and classifications. This station invited curiosity, reasoning, and rich discussion, and subtly modeled how a teacher-led group could use time differently: not to reteach content but to spark inquiry and deepen thinking through responsive facilitation.

This station rotation wasn't just a shift in structure—it was a deliberate design grounded in the principles of UDL. Each station provided multiple means of engagement, inviting students to collaborate, play, debate, or investigate—and connect with math in ways that sparked curiosity and sustained their attention. There were also multiple means of representation built into the experience: Digital tools, visuals, physical manipulatives, verbal clues, and visual vocabulary banks ensured that students could access key ideas through more than one modality. Finally, students had multiple means of action and expression. They asked questions, drew and measured shapes, constructed arguments, and explained their thinking aloud and in writing. Whether sketching to solve a mystery, justifying a claim with a peer, or revising a partner's angle measurement, each student had a chance to demonstrate understanding in a way that worked for them. This intentional design allowed all students to engage deeply with the content, regardless of readiness level, learning preference, or confidence with math—and that's the power of combining blended learning with UDL.

Together, UDL and blended learning create the conditions for deeper, more effective instruction. Blended learning models enable you to leverage technology thoughtfully, creating opportunities for differentiation and personalization while freeing yourself from the front of the room. This strategic use of technology allows more time for the human side of teaching—valuable time for working directly with students to meet them where they are, supporting their individual learning paths and fostering agency. In this way, blended learning allows you to more easily implement the updated UDL Guidelines, ensuring that all learners have access to multiple means of engagement, representation, and action and expression—all in a way that feels practical and sustainable.

Blended learning offers a practical, flexible framework that aligns with the goals of UDL by providing instructional models that give students more agency and control over their learning while allowing teachers to work with individual students or small groups to more effectively meet their needs. Blended learning provides the mindset (valuing flexibility and learner agency), the skill set (instructional models that support differentiation and personalization), and the tool set (technology and student-led learning strategies) educators need to put UDL into practice effectively.

## Summary

UDL and blended learning are powerful partners that enable educators to meet the diverse needs of their students while maintaining flexibility and sustainability in their teaching practices. UDL provides the guiding principles for recognizing and honoring learner variability, ensuring that each student can engage with content, make meaning, and express their understanding in ways that work best for them. Blended learning provides the practical framework for implementing these principles by integrating both online and offline learning, offering students more control over their learning experience while allowing teachers to focus on high-impact instructional strategies.

Shifting from traditional, teacher-centered approaches to blended learning models empowers educators to move beyond one-size-fits-all instruction. Teachers can dedicate their time and energy to strategies like differentiated small-group instruction, ongoing feedback, and one-on-one conferencing—creating more equitable learning environments that address individual student needs.

## Reflect and Discuss

1. Reflect on the reality that "variability is the norm, not the exception." How do you currently design lessons to account for student variability? In what ways do you currently incorporate flexibility in your lessons, and where might you have opportunities for growth?

2. What shifts in your mindset or practice are required to fully embrace learner agency? How might this shift from teacher control to student ownership challenge your current approach to teaching? What opportunities do you see in giving students more control over their learning paths?

3. In what ways might traditional, whole-group, teacher-led instruction fall short of supporting all of your students? Reflect on how relying on one instructional model might unintentionally create barriers to learning. How could blended learning approaches such as the Station Rotation Model help you better meet the diverse needs of your students?

4. What are the biggest barriers to implementing UDL in your classroom? How might shifting from whole-group, teacher-led lessons to small-group instruction with the Station Rotation Model help you to address some of these challenges?

5. How can you strategically use technology to free yourself from the front of the classroom? One of the advantages of blended

learning is that it allows teachers to step back from the traditional role of content delivery. Reflect on how you might use technology to give students more autonomy and what you would do with the time and space that creates.

6. How do you think co-creating learning experiences with students might impact classroom culture? The updated UDL Guidelines emphasize co-creation. How might involving students in the design of their learning experiences shift the dynamics in your classroom and increase engagement?

## Time to Apply: Restate and Create

**Objective:** Restate the UDL Guidelines in your own words and then create a list of "would you rather" options that offer your students flexible pathways for engagement, representation, and action and expression specific to your grade level and subject area.

### Step 1: Restate Each Guideline in Your Own Words

Review the three core UDL principles: engagement, representation, and action and expression. Then try the following:

- For each principle, restate the principle in language that feels natural to you and reflects your teaching context. For example, instead of "multiple means of engagement," you might say, "provide different ways for students to connect with what they're learning."
- As you restate each principle, think about how it applies specifically to your grade level and subject area. Write this down or create a visual/graphic representation.

### Step 2: Identify Key Concepts for Flexible Pathways

For each of the three UDL principles, think about how you already offer, or could offer, flexible options for students in your lessons.

Reflect on moments in your classroom where flexibility might make a difference in terms of student engagement, how they access content, and how they show what they know.

### *Step 3: Develop "Would You Rather" Options*

Now, create a list of "would you rather" options for each of the UDL Guidelines:

- **Engagement:** Consider what excites or motivates students.
- **Representation:** Think about how students best receive or engage with information.
- **Action and expression:** Offer options for how students can express or share their understanding.

Tailor these options to your subject area and grade level. For instance, a high school history class might have different options than a kindergarten class.

**CHAPTER 2**

# Understanding the Station Rotation Model

## Not All Airbnbs Are Created Equal

As a professional learning facilitator and speaker, I travel all over the country for work and often stay in an Airbnb instead of a hotel. I like the feeling of being in a home environment rather than a generic hotel. But not all Airbnbs are created equal.

On a recent trip to Virginia, I booked an Airbnb cottage attached to a house because I needed reliable Wi-Fi to present an online class. Over the years, I've stayed in Airbnbs that barely cover the basics—places with no clear instructions for check-in, unexpected stairs I had to drag my luggage up, or kitchenettes completely lacking utensils or even coffee. These kinds of stays always feel lackluster, leaving me a little frustrated and wishing the hosts had put more thought into the details.

This Virginia cottage, however, was the opposite of those experiences. From the moment I booked, it was clear the hosts had been incredibly intentional about the guest experience. The description on Airbnb was detailed and thorough. When I arrived, I knew exactly where to park and how to unlock the door thanks to a clear, step-by-step guide, including photos.

Inside, they had thought of everything. There were snacks, a bottle of wine, coffee and tea, plates, utensils, cold water in the fridge—everything I needed to feel comfortable. They'd even stocked extra toiletries: a razor, a comb, and extra soap, just in case I'd forgotten something. And there was a thoughtfully put-together booklet with Wi-Fi information, local restaurant recommendations, and a simple checklist for what to do before checking out.

That experience made me reflect on the difference between basic and intentional design. It wasn't just about having a place to sleep; it was about creating an experience where I felt welcomed, supported, and comfortable.

And that's exactly what we need to do in education. Basic design covers the essentials, but intentional design takes it further. It anticipates needs, removes obstacles, and adds those thoughtful touches that make learning more accessible, engaging, and effective. Just like my stay in Virginia, when we design learning with intention, we create environments where students can thrive.

## Firm Goals

By the end of this chapter, you will:

- Understand the benefits of the Station Rotation Model compared with the traditional whole-group, teacher-led model
- Know the difference between classic "learning centers" and the Station Rotation Model.
- Comprehend the basic design of a station rotation and the purpose of each station.
- Appreciate the elements of high-quality intentional design.

# What Is the Station Rotation Model?

The Station Rotation Model is one of several rotation models within the taxonomy of blended learning. As its name suggests, it is composed of a series of stations, or learning activities, that students rotate through. While the number and design of the stations can vary, the most common implementation includes three types of stations: teacher-led, online, and offline, as pictured in figure 2.1.

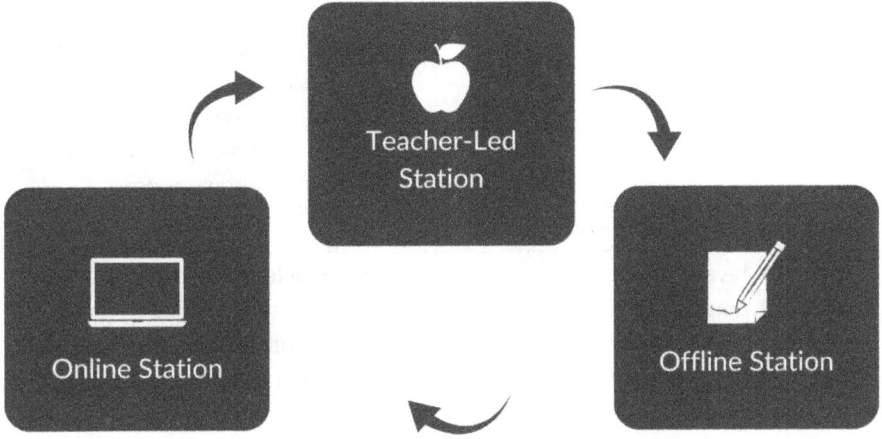

**Figure 2.1: The Basic Design of the Station Rotation Model**

Let's explore each type of station to understand its purpose and the types of learning activities that work well at that station, as described in table 2.1.

**Table 2.1: Station Types and Their Instructional Purpose**

| Purpose of the Station | Example Station Activities |
|---|---|
| **Type of Station: Teacher-led station** ||
| This station provides the teacher with the opportunity to work with a small group of students to differentiate instruction, provide targeted support, guide initial practice, facilitate dynamic discussions, give students feedback on work in progress, and check for understanding in real time. | • Differentiated direct instruction based on data or student needs<br>• Interactive and differentiated modeling of a strategy, skill, or process<br>• Guided practice with teacher coaching<br>• Formative feedback on work in progress<br>• Formative assessments to gather real-time data and adjust instruction and support |
| **Type of Station: Online station** ||
| This station leverages digital tools to allow for personalized practice, access to multimedia content, research and exploration, collaborative work, and creation with digital tools. It can provide students with greater control over the pace and path of their learning. | • Adaptive learning programs for personalized practice<br>• Multimedia lessons, such as short instructional videos or podcasts<br>• Virtual museum or gallery tours<br>• Collaborative work using shared documents or discussion boards<br>• Online research and exploration tied to an essential question or real-world connection<br>• Digital creation tools that allow students to create diverse products to demonstrate their learning |

| Type of Station: Offline station | |
|---|---|
| This station offers students a screen-free space to engage in hands-on, tactile, or interpersonal learning. It emphasizes reading, writing, speaking, listening, reflecting, and creating in ways that support meaning-making and reinforce key skills. | • Paired practice or peer feedback routines<br>• Reading passages and responding in writing<br>• Small-group discussions using conversation protocols<br>• Creating concept maps to visualize connections between ideas<br>• Thinking routines to encourage metacognition<br>• Art or maker projects to express understanding creatively |

The Station Rotation Model is designed to 1) provide teachers with dedicated time to work directly with small groups and 2) give students more control over the pace and path of their learning. However, the benefits of the Station Rotation Model extend far beyond these advantages.

# What Are the Benefits of the Station Rotation Model?

The Station Rotation Model has myriad benefits when compared with a whole-group, teacher-led, teacher-paced lesson. Here are a few of the benefits:

- **Differentiated instruction, modeling, and support:** Through the Station Rotation Model, teachers can differentiate more consistently and effectively by working with small groups, allowing us to tailor instruction, models, feedback, and support to meet the diverse needs of all our students. In this setting, teachers can model complex skills, provide targeted support, and adjust instructional strategies to accommodate varying skill levels, needs, language proficiencies, and learning preferences. This approach ensures that instruction is accessible and helps every student progress toward standards-aligned goals.

- **Collaboration and peer support:** As part of the Station Rotation Model, students frequently work together in small groups, fostering a collaborative learning environment and improving their feelings of relatedness and connection to an inclusive learning community. This encourages peer support, as students learn with and from each other. At stations, students can share ideas, provide peer feedback, and collaborate on shared tasks, enhancing their understanding and engagement.
- **Smaller learning communities:** When teachers shift from a whole-group to a small-group dynamic, they create smaller learning communities within the larger class. This gives the teacher and students more opportunities to engage with each other. Teachers feel more effective in meeting the needs of small groups, and students have more opportunities to engage with each other.
- **More opportunities for student autonomy and agency:** Students enjoy more independence in the learning environment since they have more control over the pace at which they move through the learning activities at the stations that are not teacher led. Teachers can include meaningful "would you rather" choices at the stations in a rotation, allowing students to decide how they acquire information (e.g., article versus video) or process information and make meaning (e.g., concept map or small-group discussion). Prioritizing agency in the design of a station rotation removes barriers, allowing students to select a pathway that works best for them. Research further suggests that providing students

with agency also increases their confidence in their ability to be successful, positively impacting their motivation.[1]

- **Self-regulation skills:** As students navigate through the various stations in a rotation, they develop essential self-regulation skills. They learn to manage their time, monitor their progress, and maintain focus and attention. In fact, studies from the University of Guelph's Office of Teaching and Learning suggest that the structure of the Station Rotation Model inherently promotes the development of these skills, helping students become more independent and effective learners.[2] Teaching students to manage their learning processes aligns with the UDL principle of supporting executive functions.

- **Flexible grouping:** Teachers can group students based on their instructional needs, skills, or interests. This flexibility ensures that all students receive the appropriate level of challenge and support for a given lesson. It also allows teachers to create dynamic learning environments that can adapt to their students' evolving needs, aligning with UDL's emphasis on flexibility and inclusivity. We'll explore grouping strategies in more depth in chapter 10.

## The Station Rotation Model vs. Traditional Learning Centers

Learning centers, or stations, are not new in education, so some teachers may assume they have been using the Station Rotation Model already. There are, however, a few key differences between traditional learning centers and the Station Rotation Model; namely, the Station Rotation Model integrates an online learning station, places emphasis on shifting control over pace and path to students, and uses data strategically to inform the design of learning.

In classic learning centers, students typically rotate through various activities or centers that are primarily offline and teacher directed. These activities are designed to reinforce skills and concepts but often follow a set pace and structure determined by the teacher. The tasks are usually uniform for all students without any differentiation or personalization.

The Station Rotation Model, by contrast, incorporates an online learning station, providing opportunities for personalized, adaptive learning experiences. This online component allows students to engage with interactive digital content, receive immediate feedback, and work at their own pace.

Table 2.2: Classic Learning Centers vs. the Station Rotation Model

| Classic Learning Centers | Station Rotation Model |
|---|---|
| In a third-grade classroom, the teacher sets up three learning centers to reinforce literacy skills: | In a third-grade classroom, the teacher implements the Station Rotation Model to reinforce literacy skills: |
| 1. **Reading center:** Students read a book and complete comprehension questions.<br>2. **Writing center:** Students work on writing prompts and practice their handwriting.<br>3. **Vocabulary center:** Students play a word-matching game using physical cards. | 1. **Teacher-led station:** The teacher works with a small group on reading comprehension strategies, using a text at a level that is accessible and providing individualized feedback and support.<br>2. **Online learning station:** Students use a reading program on their devices that adapts to their reading level, providing interactive exercises and instant feedback. They can progress through the content at their own pace.<br>3. **Offline station:** Students engage in a collaborative writing project, where they write and illustrate stories, sharing ideas and providing peer feedback. |

In the classic learning centers pictured in table 2.2, all students rotate through each center on a fixed schedule, spending twenty minutes at each center. The activities are the same for all students, and the teacher determines the pace and path. While students engage in different tasks, they do so simultaneously and within the same time frame. The teacher may circulate around the room answering questions and monitoring progress but may not work directly with a small group of students.

In the Station Rotation Model, students rotate through each station, but they have more control over their learning. At the online station, students can move through the reading program content at a pace that works for them and access texts at a reading level appropriate to their skills and abilities. The teacher uses data to group students strategically, so the teacher-led station allows for targeted instruction tailored to each group's specific literacy needs. The teacher can guide a small-group instructional session using texts at different levels of rigor and complexity and provide various degrees of scaffolding and support. The offline station encourages collaboration and creativity, providing students with time to work together on a shared task. This Station Rotation Model lesson blends teacher guidance with technology-enhanced learning and peer interaction.

## Basic Design vs. Intentional Design

The Station Rotation Model can be implemented in various ways, but the impact on the quality of student learning can vary significantly based on design.

For example, a basic Station Rotation Model design often involves students rotating through stations where they may still be passive recipients of information and complete review activities. At the teacher-led station, students might listen to a lecture or work through a mini-lesson, but this direct instruction may not be tailored to each group's specific needs. Students might engage with a personalized program or watch a video lesson at the online station, often working independently. The offline station may involve worksheets or other independent review activities or tasks. This basic design may lack data-informed design, differentiation, and student agency, and it is unlikely to yield high levels of student engagement or produce dramatically different academic outcomes.

By contrast, designing a Station Rotation Model with a high level of intentionality requires purpose and planning. You begin by identifying clear learning objectives aligned with standards. Then, you use a pre-assessment or access prior knowledge activity to understand where each student is beginning in relation to the concepts and skills that will be covered in a lesson or sequence of lessons. Then, you use that data to inform the design of each station and differentiate effectively. This high level of intentionality ensures that all students make meaningful progress toward the learning goals regardless of where they begin in relation to specific concepts or skills.

As we'll discuss more fully in part II of this book, key elements of intentional Station Rotation Model design include the following:

- **Data-informed instruction:** Utilize diagnostic, pre-assessment, or formative assessment data to identify the unique needs of students, ensuring instruction addresses these needs effectively.
- **Differentiated instruction:** Tailor instruction, activities, and supports to meet diverse learning needs, ensuring each station addresses different skills, abilities, learning preferences, language proficiencies, and interests.
- **Formative assessment:** Embed assessment mechanisms that provide informal data about student progress toward learning objectives and adjust instruction as needed.
- **Student agency:** Give students opportunities to make meaningful choices about their learning experience.

In table 2.3, let's look at an example of a high school biology class, comparing a basic Station Rotation Model with one that was developed with a high level of intentionality.

**Table 2.3: High School Biology Lesson—
Basic vs. Intentional Design**

| Basic Design | Intentional Design |
|---|---|
| In a high school biology class, a basic Station Rotation Model might include this: <br><br>1. **Teacher-led station:** The teacher gives a brief lecture on cell structure, with all students receiving the same information regardless of their prior knowledge.<br>2. **Online station:** Students watch a video on cell functions and fill in a guided note template.<br>3. **Offline station:** Students complete a worksheet, reviewing concepts from the previous class, working independently. | In the same high school biology class, an intentional Station Rotation Model might look like this:<br><br>1. **Teacher-led station:** Based on pre-assessment data, the teacher groups students by their understanding of cell structure. Each group receives tailored instruction that addresses their specific misconceptions and extends their knowledge with relevant information and examples.<br>2. **Online station:** Students are given a "would you rather" choice between two learning activities:<br>　○ Option 1: Read an online article about cell functions, exploring detailed descriptions and diagrams.<br>　○ Option 2: Watch a video explaining cell functions with animations and real-life applications.<br><br>After choosing either the article or videos, students select a strategy for processing and making meaning of the content:<br>• Create a concept map.<br>• Write a reflective summary.<br>• Participate in an online discussion.<br><br>3. **Offline station:** Students engage in a collaborative project where they create 3D models of cells using various materials. They can choose from different types of cells to model (e.g., plant, animal, bacterial). |

In the basic design of the biology Station Rotation Model lesson pictured in table 2.3, there is minimal differentiation, and students have limited opportunities to engage actively or take ownership of their learning. By contrast, the intentional design uses data to inform instruction, differentiates effectively, and provides students with meaningful choices. This approach positions students as active agents in the learning process and provides the teacher and peer support needed to be successful.

By approaching design with intentionality, educators can create elevated and equitable experiences that provide each student with a flexible, dynamic, and accessible learning pathway.

## Going Horizontal with Your Linear Agenda

When teachers assume they cannot use the Station Rotation Model in their class, or struggle to design stations that function independently and do not build on each other like a typical linear lesson, I share my strategy of "going horizontal."

I'm referring to the process of turning a traditional, linear lesson agenda—where each activity builds on the one before it—on its side to examine the individual components. Teachers are used to designing whole-group lessons where the sequence matters: We start with direct instruction, move into guided practice, and end with independent work. That's a linear flow. But in the Station Rotation Model, each station needs to function independently so students can rotate through them in any order.

*Going horizontal* means breaking apart that linear lesson and analyzing each learning activity to see whether it can stand alone as a station. Some stations may support the same learning objective in different ways, while others may address different standards or skill areas entirely—like reading, writing, vocabulary, and speaking. It's a shift in perspective that allows for more flexible, multidimensional lesson design.

When I designed my first few Station Rotation Model lessons, I was frustrated because my stations always built on each other. So, I returned to what I was comfortable with—the whole-group, linear agenda.

The agenda below was the first linear agenda I reimagined with the Station Rotation Model. It was a ninth-grade English lesson that addressed grade-level writing, reading, research, and speaking and listening skills. At the time, I taught on a ninety-minute block period, so a teacher with shorter class periods may need to run a multiday rotation or reduce the number of stations.

Here's the linear agenda:

- Present a mini-lesson on how to write a thesis statement.
- Read and annotate an informational text about migrant workers.
- Research the Dust Bowl to understand the historical context surrounding *Of Mice and Men*.
- Discuss chapter 3 in *Of Mice and Men*.

To adapt this agenda more meaningfully for the Station Rotation Model, I had to go horizontal by tilting the agenda on its side and pulling apart the discrete learning activities to answer two essential questions:

1. Could these individual learning activities work as learning stations with some modification?
2. Would this be a better lesson with the Station Rotation Model?

Figure 2.2 shows the Station Rotation Model lesson I created from my linear agenda. Instead of moving in lockstep through the four activities listed in my original linear agenda, I created four stations.

## The Station Rotation Model and UDL

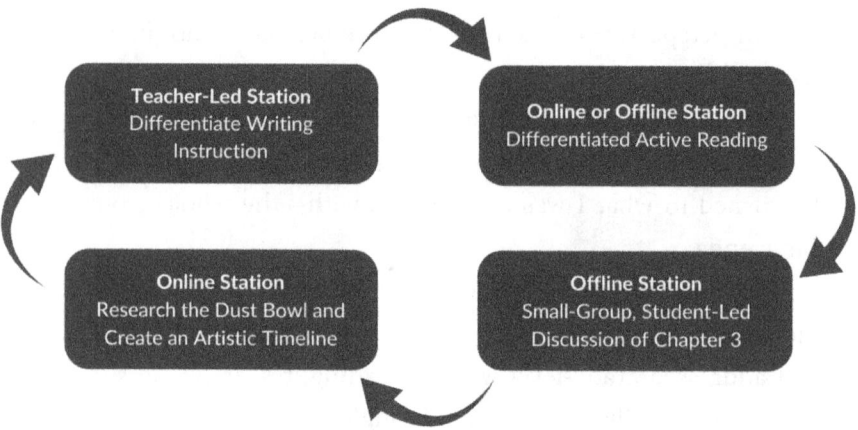

**Figure 2.2: Linear Lesson Reimagined with the Station Rotation Model**

When designing my lesson, I had to consider what benefit shifting from a whole group to a small group would have on the learning activities in my lesson.

Initially, this was a whole-group lesson with a clear linear agenda: a mini-lesson on thesis writing, followed by reading and annotating an informational text, researching the Dust Bowl, and wrapping up with a class discussion about chapter 3 in *Of Mice and Men*. Each activity built on the last, and all students moved through the same sequence together. But when I challenged myself to go horizontal, I began to see how I could break that linear sequence apart and reimagine each part as an independent station. This shift allowed me to consider how each activity could stand alone and serve a unique purpose within the Station Rotation Model. It also helped me think more strategically about how to group students, differentiate my instruction, and design for more active, student-centered engagement. What follows is a breakdown of how I transformed each part of that original linear lesson into a station and the advantages of facilitating the lesson in this format.

## Differentiated Writing Instruction

First, grouping students based on their writing skills for the day allowed me to tailor my instruction at the teacher-led station, providing various levels of support and scaffolding for each group. Here's an example:

- **High-level writers:** I challenged my stronger writers to analyze example thesis statements and engage in a collaborative challenge, identifying and listing the elements they thought made a strong thesis statement. That way, they had to think critically, engage in conversation, and collaborate with their peers to reach their conclusions before I gave the instruction. After the instruction, they transitioned to writing a draft of their thesis statements, and I provided feedback as they worked.
- **Mid-level writers:** I provided instruction on how to write a thesis statement, identify the necessary components, and model the process of writing a thesis statement, conducting a think-aloud as I wrote. Then, students transitioned to writing a draft of their thesis statements, and I spent the time we had left providing feedback.
- **Low-level writers:** Students who needed more support and scaffolding benefited from receiving explicit instruction on how to write a thesis statement and what to include, as well as seeing me model the process of writing one while conducting a think-aloud. They also benefited from a thesis statement sentence frame to support them in structuring their thesis statements. As they used the frame, I provided individual support and feedback.

By integrating instruction, guided practice, and feedback into the teacher-led station, I could more effectively differentiate the experience to meet the diverse writing needs of the students in my class. This approach also made it possible to provide the appropriate scaffolds and supports for each student.

### *Differentiated Active Reading*

Normally, in a whole-group lesson, I would find an article related to some aspect of the historical context of the novel we were reading for this activity. Traditionally, I would photocopy the same article for everyone, pass it out, and popcorn read it aloud as a class. I would pause the group at strategic moments in the reading to highlight key information, make connections, or ask questions.

This approach is problematic on a couple of levels. First, the articles were not at a reading level accessible to all the students in my class. Today, I could use Newsela to find articles on a topic written at different Lexile levels, use an AI text leveler, or provide students with a print and an audio version. I was also doing the heavy cognitive lift because I was the person thinking critically about the text and guiding students through it, highlighting all the important information.

If students had a text at a reading level they could access on their own or had the option to read or listen to an audio track, this reading activity could be done independently, with a partner at a station, or as a reciprocal teaching activity with a group. Teachers could invite students to select a strategy to actively engage with the reading—annotations, sketchnotes, guided note templates. This is an opportunity to shift control over the pace of reading to the students while also building in student agency and meaningful choice.

### *Small-Group, Student-Led Discussion*

The benefit of shifting from a whole-group, teacher-led discussion to a small-group, student-led one is that it can remove barriers to participation. In a whole-group, teacher-led discussion, there isn't time for every student to participate. It's also common for the teacher to do most of the cognitive work because they feel compelled to respond to each student's contribution by highlighting strong points made, making connections between the ideas shared, and gently correcting misconceptions.

In a small-group, student-led discussion, everyone can engage in the conversation, making it more equitable. Students who are shy or struggle with anxiety are more likely to participate in this small-group dynamic. Students may also take more risks asking questions and sharing their ideas because they know the teacher will not jump in with the "correct" answers.

These conversations help students develop their speaking and listening skills as well as their relationships with peers. Teachers can also ask students to conclude their discussion with a short self-assessment and reflection on their participation. That way, students are thinking about how they are contributing to these conversations and what goals they want to set for themselves in future discussions.

### *Research the Dust Bowl*

This activity would be ideal for an online collaborative station where a small group of students research together. As they explore this moment in history, they can capture and organize what they're learning by creating an artistic timeline on poster paper or using an online tool like Canva or Google Drawings, depending on their group's preference.

This research activity can encourage the group to communicate and collaborate as they explore this historical event. It could also be an opportunity to provide students with a meaningful choice in how they document their learning (you can give them a simple "would you rather" option).

After redesigning my linear lesson with the Station Rotation Model, I answered the two questions I started with. First, did this linear lesson work with the Station Rotation Model? Yes! I modified the individual learning activities as separate stations that blended online and offline learning as well as individual and collaborative tasks, which kept students engaged. I included student agency and meaningful choice to remove barriers and ensure that all students could successfully complete each task.

Second, was this a better lesson with the Station Rotation Model? Yes! I differentiated my instruction and support at the teacher-led station while differentiating the reading task and allowing students to have more control over the pace at which they read and engaged with the article. The research station targeted all four Cs of twenty-first-century learning: critical thinking, communication, collaboration, and creativity. The discussion station provided every student with the opportunity to share their thinking and participate.

# Dispelling Myths about the Station Rotation Model

Teachers often have misconceptions about the Station Rotation Model, so it's important to clear those up right at the start.

### Myth #1: The Station Rotation Model Is an Elementary Model

One common misconception about the Station Rotation Model is that it is only appropriate for K–5 students. This misconception may arise because elementary teachers often spend the entire day with the same group of learners, necessitating various instructional strategies to keep students engaged and learning. The Station Rotation Model helps maintain engagement with a variety of learning activities and differentiated instruction. However, like their younger counterparts, secondary students benefit from small-group instruction and differentiated learning experiences. Secondary classrooms are also composed of diverse groups of students with different skills, abilities, language proficiencies, and learning preferences, so the Station Rotation Model is equally beneficial for students from kindergarten through high school.

Secondary teachers also have a strong content-area focus or expertise, positioning them as subject matter experts. This expertise may lead teachers to dedicate significant time to direct instruction, where information is primarily presented through lectures or mini-lessons. This hierarchical approach to transferring information can make it challenging for secondary teachers to embrace the Station Rotation Model, which entails releasing control and allowing students to lead aspects of the learning. But, by rotating through different stations, students have opportunities to engage with content in multiple ways—whether through teacher-led instruction, online activities, offline tactile tasks, or collaborative projects. This variety supports different learning preferences and promotes autonomy, which is especially important for older students' motivation and their ability to hone their self-directed learning skills.

## Myth #2: There Must Be Three Stations in a Rotation

Another common misconception is that the Station Rotation Model requires three stations. The total number of stations in a rotation can vary depending on a few variables:

- **Length of class period:** If a class period is shorter, the teacher might design fewer stations to ensure students have enough time to engage meaningfully with each activity. Conversely, longer periods may accommodate more stations.
- **Time spent in each station:** Teachers must decide how much time students will spend at each station. I typically recommend twenty to twenty-five minutes, depending on the age of your students. The goal is to balance engagement and productivity, ensuring students have sufficient time to

engage deeply with the tasks and materials without feeling rushed.
- **Group size:** Smaller groups can lead to more personalized attention and better engagement, while larger groups might be necessary due to classroom constraints. Adjusting the number of stations can help manage group sizes effectively. However, you can also strategically pair students or create "pods" at a station, essentially creating smaller groups within the station to lower the number of students working together.

In short, the Station Rotation Model is versatile and can be adapted to fit various classroom settings, lengths, and student needs.

## *Myth #3: My Classes Are Too Short to Use the Station Rotation Model*

Another common misconception is that the Station Rotation Model cannot be used in a traditional middle or high school period of forty-five or fifty minutes. However, teachers can design multiday rotations to accommodate shorter periods. For example, a two-day, four-station schedule can begin with a welcome activity, after which students rotate through two stations. On the second day, they rotate through the remaining two stations. This approach ensures that all stations are covered without the pressure of completing the rotation in a single class period.

Let's explore an example in a high school history class with a fifty-minute period. The teacher wants to run a two-day rotation with four stations. On day one, students will visit two stations, and on day two, they will complete the remaining two stations.

- **Station 1 (teacher-led):** Facilitate a small-group discussion of primary source documents, focusing on guiding analysis and interpretation. The teacher can select sources at different levels of vigor and complexity and have scaffolds like word banks, sentence stems, and deconstructed examples available.

- **Station 2 (online):** Students choose between reading an article on a historical event or watching part of a video documentary, then create a concept map or participate in an online discussion.
- **Station 3 (online/offline):** Collaborative project where students conduct research on a specific time period and collaborate to create a shared timeline offline with posters and pens or online with a tool like Google Drawing or Canva.
- **Station 4 (offline):** Students role-play historical figures, debating key issues from their perspectives. They finish by capturing their reflections in writing or a concept map.

In this example, the rotation is spread over two days, with students completing the work at two stations each day. This flexible approach allows the teacher to maximize class time, provide a variety of learning experiences, and cater to different learning preferences.

No rule book mandates the completion of a rotation within one class period. This flexibility allows teachers to implement the Station Rotation Model regardless of class length.

## Myth #4: My Classes Are Too Large to Use the Station Rotation Model

A common concern among teachers with large class sizes is that the Station Rotation Model requires small groups and, therefore, won't work in a crowded classroom. Teachers often worry that creating enough stations for all students or managing behavior in a larger group setting will be too overwhelming.

The Station Rotation Model is adaptable, even in classrooms with large numbers of students. Teachers can use a "mirror station" design to address these challenges while maintaining the benefits of small-group learning. Instead of planning six or more unique stations to accommodate a large class, teachers can design three stations and divide the room into two halves, with each half of the room rotating through mirror, or identical, stations.

Here's why and how the mirror station variation works:

- **Reduces planning time:** By using the same set of stations for both sides of the room, the teacher significantly decreases the amount of front-loading required to plan the lesson. This simplifies preparation while still providing variety and engagement for students.
- **Creates smaller groups:** Even with a large class, this approach reduces the number of students at each station, creating a more focused and productive learning environment.
- **Allows for a teacher-led station:** If the teacher wants to provide direct instruction or model a process, they can plan for the teacher-led station to be larger, with two groups converging at this station during each rotation. By carefully structuring the activity, the teacher can ensure that every student gets the necessary support while fostering collaboration and accountability among peers.

The Station Rotation Model doesn't require perfect conditions to be effective—it thrives on flexibility. Using strategies like mirror stations, teachers can transform even the largest classes into dynamic, student-centered learning environments. With thoughtful planning, this model becomes not only manageable but also an opportunity to create more personalized learning experiences for every student.

## Myth #5: The Station Rotation Model Won't Work with My Subject Area

A frequent misconception is that the Station Rotation Model is not a good fit for subject areas like math, where lessons are often viewed

## Understanding the Station Rotation Model

as a linear progression from mini-lesson to practice. However, this perspective underestimates the model's flexibility and limits our ability to reimagine math instruction to better meet all students' instructional needs.

The reality is that the Station Rotation Model works beautifully in math classrooms when teachers rethink how they design and structure their time. Instead of relying on a single flow—an "I do, we do" mini-lesson, followed by "you do" practice—the teacher-led station can take on a new role, presenting fresh content or skills each day at the teacher-led station while the other stations serve complementary purposes.

For example, a math instructor might implement the Station Rotation Model in this way:

- **Teacher-led station:** Use this time to introduce a new concept or skill in a small-group setting where the teacher can differentiate instruction using problems at different levels of complexity to ensure students understand the new material. In a small teacher-led group, students also benefit from personalized support and immediate feedback.
- **Practice station:** Students can engage in spiral review, practicing skills or concepts introduced in earlier lessons. This station provides opportunities for spaced practice, which is critical for retention and mastery.[3]
- **Video station:** A video lesson can prime students for what's coming next, setting them up for success in future lessons by providing a preview of concepts, processes, or vocabulary.
- **Collaborative station:** Give students time to apply their math skills to real-world problems, solve challenges together, or explore tasks that encourage transfer, creative problem-solving, and teamwork.

The Station Rotation Model doesn't prevent math teachers from meeting their instructional goals; it simply requires a shift in thinking. Teachers can use stations to design experiences that are more flexible, more dynamic, and better tailored to their students' needs. By breaking free from the idea that math lessons must follow a rigid sequence each day, teachers open up opportunities to revisit, reinforce, and apply concepts to make learning more meaningful and engaging.

Any shift in our practice or the way we design lessons is daunting. You may have believed some of the myths covered in this chapter or struggled to conceptualize your linear lessons as a circular rotation. The good news is that with some practice, these challenges are not insurmountable obstacles. As you work through this book, you will discover how this model can improve the quality of your lessons and result in higher levels of engagement for you and your students!

## Summary

The Station Rotation Model offers significant benefits for both elementary and secondary students by providing differentiated instruction, increasing student autonomy, and fostering the development of self-regulation skills. This model involves rotating students through teacher-led, online, and offline stations. Despite common misconceptions, this model is effective across all grade levels, adaptable to different class lengths and sizes, and flexible in the total number of stations a teacher designs. By implementing this model with intentionality, teachers can create engaging and effective learning environments that cater to the diverse needs of all students.

## Reflect and Discuss

1. What barriers to learning have you observed in your classroom during whole-group, teacher-led instruction?

How might the Station Rotation Model help address these barriers?
2. Reflect on a time when you felt overwhelmed by the diverse needs of your students. How could the Station Rotation Model have helped you manage and meet these needs more effectively?
3. Consider the balance of online and offline activities in your current teaching practice. How can the Station Rotation Model help you integrate technology in a meaningful and purposeful way?
4. Reflect on the common misconceptions about the Station Rotation Model discussed in this chapter. Which misconceptions did you previously hold, and how has this chapter impacted your thinking?
5. Think about the subjects and grade levels you teach. How could you adapt the Station Rotation Model to fit the specific needs and constraints of your classroom?

## Time to Apply: Transform a Traditional Lesson into a Station Rotation

**Objective:** Take a traditional whole-group lesson you've used in the past and go horizontal, redesigning it using the Station Rotation Model.

### Step 1: Select a Lesson

Choose a traditional, whole-group lesson you've used but felt was not as successful as you had hoped.

### Step 2: Analyze the Lesson

Break down the lesson into its key components. Identify the main instructional activities, materials, and assessments used in the lesson.

## Step 3: Redesign with the Station Rotation Model

Follow the blueprint below to transform your lesson:

- **Teacher-led station:** Identify the part of the lesson that would benefit from direct instruction, modeling, or targeted support. Plan a small-group activity where you can provide differentiated instruction and immediate feedback.
- **Online station:** Choose an activity from the lesson that could be enhanced with technology. Consider creating an interactive online component, such as a video lesson with embedded questions, a digital simulation, or a research activity that provides background. Include options for students to choose how they engage with the content (e.g., "would you rather" choices between reading an article or watching a video).
- **Offline station:** Design an offline activity that encourages hands-on learning, collaboration, or critical thinking. This could be a group project, a hands-on experiment, or a discussion-based activity.

## Step 4: Seek Peer Feedback

Find a colleague to provide you with feedback on your lesson. Do they suggest any adjustments or modifications to your Station Rotation Model lesson? Use the feedback you receive to edit and refine your lesson.

CHAPTER 3

# Elevating Tier 1 Instruction with the Station Rotation Model

## The TA Miracle

At UCLA, I had to take an introductory statistics class, and let's just say math has never been my strongest subject. I chose a statistics and political science course, hoping the political science portion would carry me through—no such luck. From day one, I found myself in a lecture hall packed with a hundred other undergrads, staring at a whiteboard filled with scribbled equations and graphs that might as well have been hieroglyphs. Despite my frantic note-taking, I left every lecture feeling more lost than the last.

What saved me wasn't the lectures but the small-group sessions led by the graduate teaching assistant (TA) assigned to a small subsection of the class. These sessions with my small group of twelve were a lifeline. My TA was not only a statistics wizard but also a fantastic teacher. He adjusted his explanations, broke down the complex concepts in ways that made sense, and provided examples (lots and lots of examples!) that helped clarify the concepts and processes our group was struggling with from the last lecture. He encouraged us to ask questions, gave real-time feedback, encouraged us to practice together, and didn't move on until we all felt confident in what we were doing.

In my small-group TA sessions, the class material actually clicked and made sense. The intimidating equations from the lectures transformed into understandable problems. My TA could see where the other members of the group and I were getting stuck, and he adapted his explanations and instruction to meet our needs, offering personalized support and guidance that would have been impossible in the massive lecture hall.

This experience taught me a powerful lesson: Small-group instruction has the potential to transform learning. While the lectures were designed for the masses, the small-group sessions were tailored to the individuals within them. That's where the magic happened—where I felt seen, supported, and capable of mastering material that had once seemed hopelessly out of reach.

Educators can provide the same small-group magic using the Station Rotation Model to improve the effectiveness of Tier 1 instruction, especially when it comes to concepts, skills, and processes that are particularly complex, nuanced, or challenging.

## Firm Goals

By the end of this chapter, you will:

- Understand the barriers that make it challenging for students to acquire new information when it is presented to the whole class in the form of a mini-lesson or lecture.
- Appreciate the difference between Tier 1, Tier 2, and Tier 3 instruction.

- Comprehend the possibilities the Station Rotation Model offers for elevating Tier 1 instruction by differentiating the presentation of information and modeling of skills to small groups.
- Grasp the opportunities the Station Rotation Model provides for Tier 2 and Tier 3 instruction.
- Gain familiarity with specific strategies co-teachers can leverage to maximize their impact when using the Station Rotation Model.

## Whole-Group Instruction: Barriers to Accessing Information

Despite its limitations, whole-group instruction remains the go-to strategy for many educators. It's deeply embedded in our collective understanding of what teaching looks like—one teacher, one whiteboard, one message delivered to the entire class. There's a certain comfort in this approach, both culturally and practically. It feels efficient. It allows teachers to maintain control and ensure that everyone receives the same information at the same time. And, in many ways, it reflects how most of us were taught. The "sage on the stage" trope is hard to shake because it's familiar and often feels necessary, especially when time is tight or when teachers are expected to cover a lot of content.

But familiarity and efficiency don't necessarily equal effectiveness. Designing with intentionality for a diverse group of learners is undeniably more challenging than delivering a one-size-fits-all lesson. However, if we say we value equity, access, and meaningful learning for all students, then the traditional whole-group approach makes it difficult, if not impossible, to live those values. While whole-group instruction may feel like the easiest way to manage a class or deliver content, it rarely accounts for the wide range of needs, abilities, interests, and prior knowledge students bring to the room. That's the heart of the problem—whole-group instruction is designed for the "mythical middle" student and tends to treat students as a single audience, rather than a collection of individual learners. To design more inclusive and equitable classrooms, we need to rethink this default and ask ourselves what barriers this format creates.

The potential barriers that may interfere with a student's ability to acquire information in this whole-group setting include:

- Hearing or sight impairments
- Attention deficit and focus challenges
- Cognitive overload
- The pace of delivery (too fast or too slow)
- Insufficient background knowledge
- Sensory overload in the classroom
- Distractions in the classroom
- Trauma or anxiety
- Limited opportunities for movement
- Language or vocabulary barriers for multilingual students
- Lack of academic or subject-specific vocabulary
- Physical or health issues (e.g., fatigue, hunger, or chronic health conditions)

These are just some of the barriers if students are physically present—this does not even account for our students who are absent, which is an increasing issue for many schools.[1] In addition to these specific barriers, whole-group instruction poses more generalized challenges that make it difficult to meet the diverse needs of all students. One major issue is that it typically offers the same instruction for every student, regardless of their individual needs, skills, or language proficiencies. This one-size-fits-all approach doesn't account for the vast range of readiness levels in the classroom, leaving some students struggling to keep up while others remain bored and unchallenged.

Whole-group instruction also positions learners as passive receivers of information, limiting their engagement with the content. When students aren't encouraged to explore, discover, or make meaning actively, their learning can be superficial. Moving at the teacher's pace also limits students' ability to process information at their own speed, making it harder for students who need more time to understand new concepts fully. Ultimately, whole-group instruction lacks the flexibility required to create meaningful, differentiated learning experiences that meet the needs of *all* learners.

As we will explore in chapter 6, differentiation involves tailoring content, process, products, and the learning environment to address the varied readiness levels, interests, and learning profiles of our students.[2] This is much easier to do when teachers can work with a smaller subset of the larger class. The Station Rotation Model simplifies effective and consistent differentiation as students move through learning activities in groups rather than as a whole class.

Importantly, differentiation doesn't need to happen everywhere all at once. When working with teachers, I emphasize starting with differentiation at the teacher-led station. This ensures that teachers consistently tailor their instruction and support before worrying about differentiating the learning activities at all the other stations. Once they are consistently designing their teacher-led station with specific groups of students in mind, they can expand this work to the other stations.

## Multi-Tiered System of Supports

Differentiation, while essential for meeting the diverse needs of learners, can feel overwhelming for many instructors. The idea of tailoring instruction for students working at different levels, with varied interests and learning preferences, often raises concerns about time, capacity, and manageability. Many teachers were not trained in how to design or facilitate differentiated learning experiences and may lack access to planning tools, peer support, or concrete instructional models. As a result, the concept of differentiation can feel more aspirational than practical. That's why frameworks like multi-tiered system of supports (MTSS) are so critical—not just for guiding student support but for supporting teachers in developing a more intentional, data-informed approach to differentiation.

MTSS is an instructional framework that uses assessment data to identify and address students' academic, behavioral, and social-emotional needs. It provides targeted instruction, scaffolds, and support at varying levels of intensity to ensure all students receive an equitable learning experience and can make progress toward clear, standards-aligned goals.[3]

Let's think of the three tiers of MTSS, pictured in figure 3.1, like the health care system.

Tier 1 is preventive care, which includes things like regular checkups designed to keep everyone healthy and spot problems early. This is similar to the high-quality, standards-aligned core instruction that all students receive.

Tier 2 is akin to visiting a specialist for targeted care, like going to physical therapy or receiving a dietary consultation. It is extra support tailored to people's specific needs that are not met in Tier 1. In education, Tier 2 entails strategies like small-group reteaching and support with specific scaffolds.

Tier 3 is intensive care, like managing a chronic condition or having surgery to correct a serious medical issue. In a classroom, Tier 3 interventions are individualized, specific, and designed to support students with the most significant academic needs.

Many educators and district-adopted curriculum present Tier 1 instruction for the whole class and rely on Tier 2 and Tier 3 interventions to work with students for whom Tier 1 was ineffective. However, if we can improve the effectiveness of Tier 1 instruction, we can reduce the need for Tier 2 or Tier 3 interventions. With that intervention in mind, then, the bulk of this chapter (and book) focuses on strategies for elevating Tier 1 instruction using differentiated small-group instruction as the vehicle.

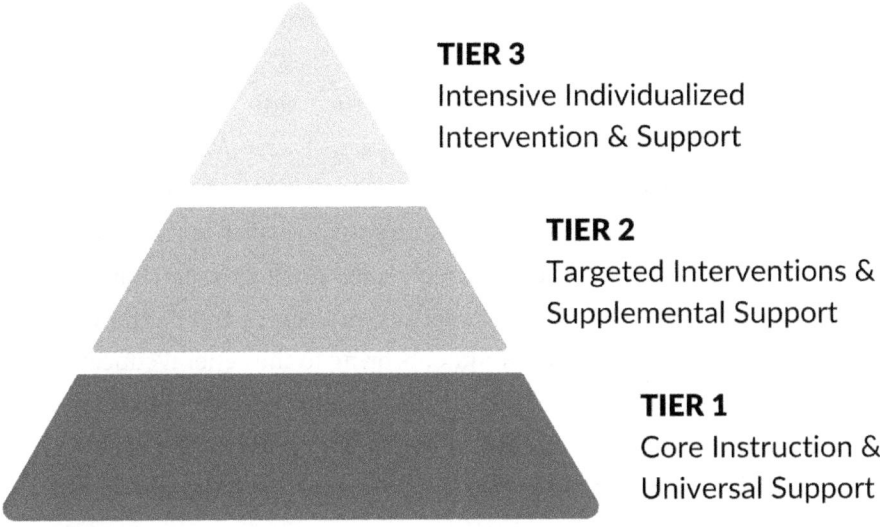

**Figure 3.1: Multi-Tiered System of Supports**

## Elevating Tier 1 Instruction

Current scholarship underscores the urgent need for the reframing of Tier 1 instruction as the ideal opportunity for differentiation. My good friend and frequent co-author, Dr. Katie Novak, emphasizes the importance of Tier 1 instruction on her podcast, *The Education Table*, explaining that "MTSS focuses heavily on creating strong Tier 1 instruction, which is the first and best instruction for all students. Research indicates that the need for additional interventions decreases significantly when Tier 1 is robust and inclusive. So, the most important component of MTSS is a strong foundation in Tier 1."[4] We must stop viewing differentiation as something reserved for interventions or small pullout groups. Instead, we need to design Tier 1 instruction—what every student receives—with the assumption that learners will need different levels of support and challenge. When we shift to blended, student-centered models like the Station Rotation Model, we create the structure and space needed to differentiate meaningfully within the core learning experience, not outside of it.

In their paper titled "Aligning Practice with Research: Using Small Groups to Differentiate Instruction," Sarah W. Siegal, Colby Hall, and Michael P. Mesa concur, arguing that "All students should receive Tier 1 instruction that includes high-quality teaching practices." They assert, "Differentiation using small groups should be considered one of those best practices and serves as a method for addressing the various needs students bring to the general education classroom." They highlight the benefits of tailoring Tier 1 instruction and support to smaller groups of students to improve the effectiveness of Tier 1 instruction. That way, we don't have the need for as many Tier 2 or Tier 3 interventions.

In a general education classroom, most instruction is presented to the whole class. The explanations, models, and scaffolds are uniform, providing all students with the same experience. Traditional instruction may follow a general curriculum plan or be teacher designed but may not include scaffolding, differentiation, or a structured, sequenced learning pathway. Traditional instruction may assume prior knowledge and language proficiencies. Often, information is delivered as a lecture that positions students to receive passively, and feedback may be infrequent or delayed. These are not aspects of high-quality Tier 1 instruction.

By contrast, high-quality Tier 1 instruction needs to be:

1. **Systematic:** Tier 1 instruction is clearly structured and breaks concepts and skills down into sequential steps, ensuring that learning builds gradually and with the necessary support. It establishes clear objectives and provides a sequence of lessons designed to guide students to those desired learning outcomes.
2. **Explicit:** Tier 1 instruction is explicit. Teachers explain concepts clearly and model skills and strategies so students can see them being applied. Then, students have ample opportunities to practice, receive guidance, and complete informal assessments to demonstrate their understanding or abilities.
3. **Data-informed:** Tier 1 instruction should be data-informed, as we will explore further in chapter 5. Teachers collect and use data to identify student needs and ensure they address them with appropriate instruction.
4. **Differentiated:** Tier 1 instruction uses data to differentiate instruction and modeling so that they meet the needs of all students in a class. Incorporating UDL principles, teachers who provide high-quality Tier 1 instruction adjust the way students access course content, process new information, and create products that demonstrate their learning.

High-quality Tier 1 instruction is intentional, inclusive, and adaptive, ensuring all students, not just some, are actively engaged and supported in making progress toward standards-aligned goals.

Many in education assume that because Tier 1 is designed to meet the needs of most students in a class, it should be presented in a teacher-led, whole-group instructional session. However, research shows that whole-group instruction is not always the most effective way to meet the needs of diverse learners. A teacher-led, one-size-fits-all approach to instruction may fail to engage all students, particularly when their readiness levels, interests, and learning profiles vary significantly. Studies on instructional grouping also highlight that students in K–12 who are grouped based on their academic needs experience improved performance outcomes.[5]

It's important to consider where and how differentiation might make a difference in your own Tier 1 instruction. When working with teachers, I encourage them to consider the following questions when deciding whether an instructional session would be better presented in differentiated small groups instead of to the whole class:

- Is this concept or skill foundational? Is it something you will need to build on instructionally?
- Is this a concept or skill that is complex, nuanced, or traditionally challenging for students to understand or apply?
- Is this a vocabulary-rich lesson that multilingual students might struggle with? Does this instruction include subject- or domain-specific vocabulary that may be challenging?
- Does the pre-assessment or diagnostic data reveal that students are in different places in relation to this concept or skill?

If the answer to any of these questions is yes, that instruction will likely be much more effective if you can present the material in a differentiated small-group instructional session. When teachers have the time to work with small groups, they can be more strategic about how they introduce concepts or model skills.

*When teachers have the time to work with small groups, they can be more strategic about how they introduce concepts or model skills.*

# Improving Tier 1 Instruction through Small-Group, Teacher-Led Stations

One of the most significant advantages of using the Station Rotation Model is its potential to enhance Tier 1 instruction to meet most students' needs in a classroom. In a traditional whole-group setting, it is challenging to meet the diverse needs of every learner with one explanation, or to model a skill at a level that works for all students. This leads to gaps in understanding and the need for more Tier 2 or even Tier 3 interventions.

But by moving Tier 1 instruction into small groups, the teacher-led station in a Station Rotation Model can differentiate to ensure the instruction is presented accessibly. Small-group differentiated instruction within the Station Rotation Model is a research-backed best practice that makes differentiation more manageable and effective within Tier 1, allowing teachers to meet diverse learner needs without pulling students out of the core learning experience.

In the teacher-led station of the Station Rotation Model, you can:

- Use texts, prompts, and/or problems at different levels of rigor and complexity
- Present core concepts in a smaller, more focused environment where you can monitor students' understanding in real time
- Provide supports and scaffolds (e.g., visual aids, graphic organizers, manipulatives)
- Adjust your instruction based on real-time formative assessment data, ensuring that students are more likely to grasp essential concepts and skills without needing further intervention
- Pair students strategically for "pairs do" activities and practice, allowing for peer support while you observe to assess

competency level and identify students who need more support
- Offer targeted scaffolds, examples, and personalized support to ensure all students have a solid foundation before moving on to more complex tasks
- Encourage students to engage in active learning, asking questions and applying skills with teacher support instead of passively receiving information and taking notes in a whole-group setting
- Adjust teacher guidance and support
- Provide timely, actionable, formative feedback

This personalized approach to Tier 1 instruction can help more students understand and apply skills during core instruction, reducing the need for Tier 2 and Tier 3 interventions. Instead of waiting for students to struggle and require additional support, the teacher-led station allows educators to identify and address learning gaps early, providing targeted instruction and individualized support. This ensures that students who might otherwise struggle in a whole-class setting are more engaged, supported, and successful during Tier 1 instruction.

---

*Instead of waiting for students to struggle and require additional support, the teacher-led station allows educators to identify and address learning gaps early, providing targeted instruction and individualized support.*

---

# Making Time for Tier 2 and Tier 3 Intervention in a Station Rotation Lesson

While I've made the case that the Station Rotation Model allows for fantastic opportunities to differentiate Tier 1 instruction, the teacher-led station is also a flexible space where you can address a range of student needs across Tiers 1, 2, and 3. During a station rotation, the teacher might deliver Tier 1 instruction aligned with grade-level standards, offer Tier 2 targeted support to small groups of students who need extra help mastering specific concepts or skills, or provide intensive individualized Tier 3 interventions.

By differentiating the focus of the teacher-led station based on student data and learning needs, you can ensure that every learner receives the personalized instruction they need to make meaningful progress. This flexibility also allows you to meet the diverse needs of learners within the same lesson structure without having to remove students from the classroom for intervention.

Additionally, the Station Rotation Model teaches students valuable self-directed and collaborative learning skills, as we'll discuss more in chapter 9. Stations can engage students in meaningful, independent tasks, such as applying concepts, practicing skills, exploring content, or engaging in reflective and metacognitive work. Collaborative stations encourage peer-to-peer learning, discussion skills, interpersonal skills, and problem-solving.

These structured learning activities free you to step away from the rotation at times. Instead of leading a teacher-led station, you can pull small groups for Tier 2 or Tier 3 interventions while the rest of the class progresses through the rotation. By leveraging students' ability to work independently and collaboratively as part of the Station Rotation Model, you create space for focused, data-informed instruction without disturbing the overall flow of the class. This approach supports intervention and fosters critical skills like autonomy, self-management, and teamwork.

In today's education landscape, the emphasis on inclusion and creating the least restrictive environments has reshaped classroom dynamics. This shift has led many schools and districts to invest in co-teaching models, where general and special education teachers or teaching assistants work together to meet the diverse needs of their students. However, without a flexible instructional approach that utilizes the talents of both teachers, co-teaching can result in a lackluster experience for both the teachers and the students. The Station Rotation Model presents opportunities for co-teachers to work in concert, providing targeted, differentiated, and personalized instruction and support.

Noelle Gutierrez and I co-authored a blog post titled "Creating Inclusive Classrooms with Co-Teaching and the Station Rotation" that explored five ways co-teachers can use the Station Rotation Model to maximize their impact in a classroom and create more inclusive learning experiences. From running two teacher-led stations to having one teacher provide differentiated Tier 1 instruction while the other pulls individual students or small groups for intervention, these strategies help co-teachers work together more effectively to meet all students' needs in a general education class.[6]

Implementing the Station Rotation Model in a co-teaching classroom can help create an inclusive environment where students of varying abilities can learn together while still receiving the targeted support they need. The model increases opportunities for differentiated and personalized instruction, allowing co-teachers to combine their strengths and address the unique needs of each student, including the goals listed on IEPs. As inclusive practices continue to shape our educational system, the Station Rotation Model provides a flexible and effective approach for meeting the diverse needs of students in the least restrictive environment.

## Summary

The Station Rotation Model can be used to deliver differentiated Tier 1 instruction while also creating opportunities for Tier 2 and Tier 3 interventions. Educators can use the teacher-led station and rotation design to provide instruction and support tailored to students' needs, ranging from core instruction to targeted small-group support or individual interventions. There is also a range of effective co-teaching strategies that can be integrated into a Station Rotation Model lesson to maximize the impact of having two adults in the room facilitating learning experiences.

## Reflect and Discuss

1. How do you currently approach Tier 1 instruction in your class? Do you present it for the whole group or in small groups? How do you differentiate instruction to ensure all of your students can access the concepts and skills presented?
2. How might using the Station Rotation Model impact your approach to providing Tier 1 instruction for concepts and skills that are complex or challenging?
3. Think about your next unit of study. What concepts and skills are complex, nuanced, or particularly challenging for students? Would it make more sense to present that material in small, teacher-led instructional sessions? Why or why not?
4. How often do you identify students who need Tier 2 or Tier 3 interventions? How do you currently provide the needed interventions? How might you use the Station Rotation Model to make time for Tier 2 and Tier 3 interventions in your classroom?
5. How can the Station Rotation Model help address equity issues in your classroom and ensure all students, regardless

of their starting point, receive the support they need to progress toward standards-aligned learning goals?
6. If you have access to a co-teacher, how could you divide responsibilities at the stations to maximize support for students? What roles might each teacher take on to ensure success at both teacher-led and independent stations?

## Time to Apply: Identify, Analyze, and Design

**Objective:** Identify a challenging concept or skill in your curriculum, analyze the diverse needs of your students, and design a differentiated small-group approach that includes specific strategies for scaffolding, practice, and extension.

### Step 1: Select a Challenging Concept or Skill

Reflect on your curriculum. Identify a concept or skill that is:

- Complex or multi-step in nature
- Frequently misunderstood by students
- A foundational building block for future learning

### Step 2: Analyze Your Students' Needs

Think about the range of abilities and prior knowledge in your class:

- What do your students typically struggle with when learning this concept or skill?
- Are there groups of students with similar needs (e.g., students who need additional scaffolding or students who could extend their understanding)?

### Step 3: Reimagine the Instruction

Consider how you would typically teach this concept or skill to the whole class. Then consider these questions:

- What could you change or adapt if you were teaching this to a small group instead of the whole class?
- How might you use visuals, manipulatives, or step-by-step modeling to support different groups?

## Step 4: Differentiate for Small Groups

Design a specific approach for at least three groups:

- **Group 1:** Students who need additional scaffolding to understand the basics.
- **Group 2:** Students ready to practice and apply the concept with minimal support.
- **Group 3:** Students who have mastered the basics and are ready for extension or enrichment.

For each group, consider:

- The level of support or scaffolding they might need.
- How you might adjust materials, examples, or tasks to meet their needs.

## Step 5: Reflect and Refine

Reflect using the following questions:

- How does this differentiated plan change the way you approach Tier 1 instruction?
- What challenges or barriers do you anticipate, and how might you address them?
- How will you assess the success of your reimagined Tier 1 instruction?

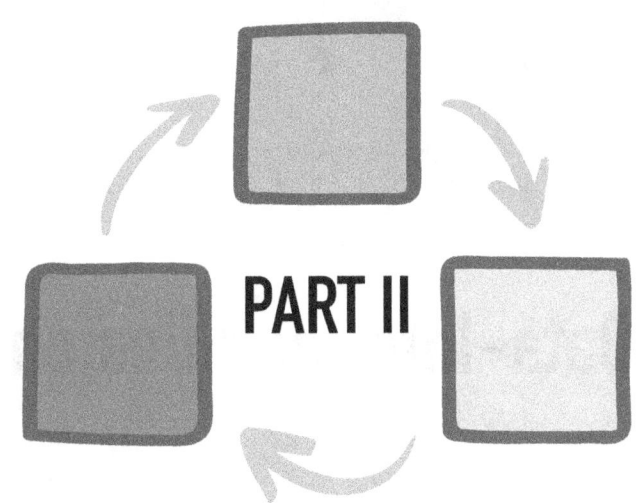

# IMPLEMENTING THE STATION ROTATION MODEL

## CHAPTER 4

# Data-Informed Design

### A Road Trip Full of Delightful Data-Informed Detours!

The spring break of my daughter's junior year of high school was the perfect opportunity for a mommy-daughter trip to check out colleges on the East Coast. We decided to make it a memorable adventure, flying into Philadelphia, renting a car, and spending six days driving north from one campus to the next, all the way to Boston Logan Airport for our evening flight home. This trip wasn't just about exploring potential colleges—it became a real-life exercise in using data to make informed decisions, both in the planning stages and as we navigated the unexpected challenges along the way.

Before we left home, we meticulously gathered all the essential data to plan our route. We researched the colleges, carefully mapping out the most efficient path to visit each one within our limited time. We used Waze to check out traffic patterns and estimated driving times between destinations, making sure to avoid rush hour in major cities. We also checked the weather forecast for each day, noting potential rainstorms or other conditions that might require us to adjust our plans.

As we hit the road, we quickly realized that having a plan was just the beginning. Much like in the classroom, where formative assessments help guide instruction, the data we gathered along the way allowed us to make real-time adjustments to our itinerary. On our third day, for instance, a major traffic jam on the interstate threatened to make us late for our campus tour in New Haven. Thanks to Waze, we identified the delay early and rerouted through scenic backroads, arriving just in time for our scheduled tour.

We also relied on other data sources throughout the trip to enhance our experience. We Googled restaurants and read online reviews to find the best local eateries, ensuring we enjoyed some yummy meals. The Starbucks app became our go-to for identifying coffee stops, providing a bit of extra energy to sustain us during the long drives. These small but important decisions were all informed by the latest available information and made the journey more enjoyable and less stressful.

By the time we reached Boston Logan Airport, we had visited every college on our list, made some spontaneous yet meaningful detours, and arrived in plenty of time for our flight home. The success of our trip was a direct result of the data we collected both before and during our journey, allowing us to make informed decisions at every turn.

In the same way, this chapter will explore how using data effectively in your classroom can help you make informed decisions about your teaching. Just as our road trip was shaped by the data we gathered and responded to, your instruction can be guided by the information you collect about your students' learning. Whether it's before a lesson or in the middle of one, data allows you to adjust your approach, ensuring that every student reaches their learning destination successfully.

## Firm Goals

By the end of this chapter, you will understand the purpose and value of using the Data-Informed Design Cycle in creating effective, differentiated instruction.

## Teaching by Design

As we discussed in part I, the Station Rotation Model presents an exciting opportunity to combine active, engaged learning—both online and offline—making it possible for us, as educators, to create more flexible and responsive learning experiences that cater to the diverse needs of our learners. This blend of offline and online learning in the classroom fosters greater student autonomy and encourages engagement by meeting students where they are in terms of skill level and learning preferences.

To fully realize the potential of the Station Rotation Model, though, educators must leverage technology effectively and use data strategically. Technology is a powerful tool to facilitate personalized learning pathways, providing students access to various resources and learning opportunities beyond the confines of the traditional classroom. However, technology alone isn't a silver bullet. The real magic happens when we combine these technological tools with insightful data analysis to inform our instructional design and decision-making processes.

Accordingly, data-informed design lies at the heart of effective implementation of the Station Rotation Model. By systematically collecting and analyzing student performance, engagement, and progress data, teachers can gain deep insights into each learner's unique strengths, challenges, and needs. This information empowers educators to tailor instruction, adjust pacing, and provide targeted support, ensuring all students progress toward clear, standards-aligned learning goals.

*Technology is a powerful tool to facilitate personalized learning pathways, providing students access to various resources and learning opportunities beyond the confines of the traditional classroom. However, technology alone isn't a silver bullet. The real magic happens when we combine these technological tools with insightful data analysis to inform our instructional design and decision-making processes.*

In practice, this means using data both as a proactive guide for instructional planning and as a retrospective measure of progress. Whether through formative assessments, learning analytics from online platforms, or observational data gathered during classroom activities, these insights enable teachers to create more responsive and adaptive learning experiences. This approach fosters a more inclusive and equitable classroom where every student has the support and resources they need to succeed.

## The Data-Informed Design Cycle

The Data-Informed Design Cycle, pictured in figure 4.1, is designed to help you make more strategic and effective instructional decisions in a blended learning environment. This cycle includes five key phases: pre-assessment, universal design with blended learning models, formative assessment, differentiated and personalized learning experiences, and summative assessment. While the cycle presents them as a linear sequence, these phases are interconnected, creating a continuous loop that ensures your teaching is responsive to the needs of all students and aligns with clear learning goals.

In the coming chapters, we'll explore how each of these phases in the Data-Informed Design Cycle ties into the process of designing

# The Station Rotation Model and UDL

the components that make up a successful Station Rotation Model. Let's review the parts of the design cycle.

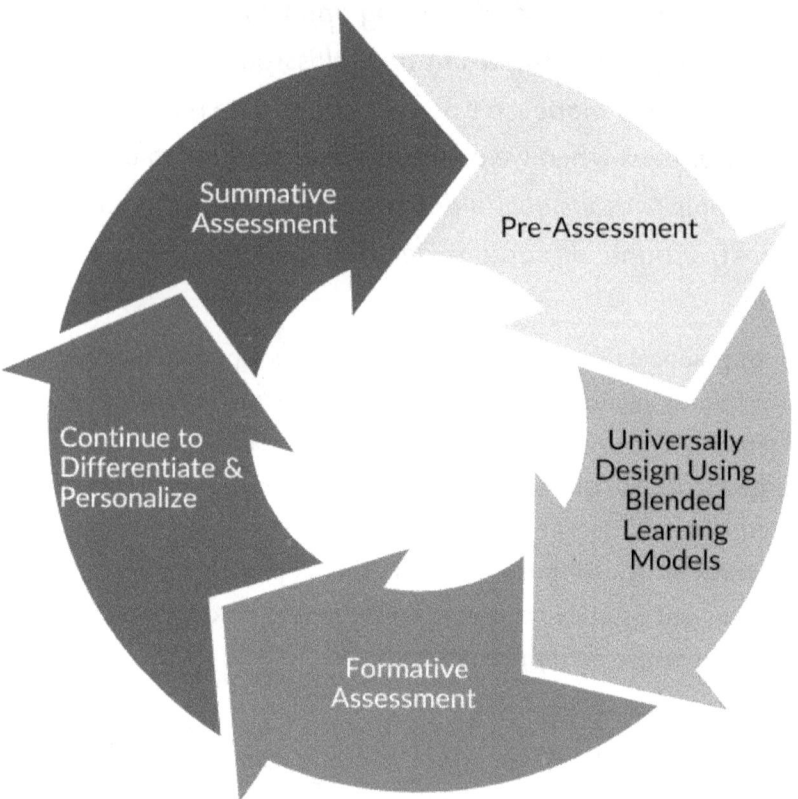

**Figure 4.1: Data-Informed Design Cycle**

1. **Pre-assessment (chapter 5):** You need to know your students' starting point to determine an effective path forward. This phase involves gathering initial data *before* instruction begins. By identifying students' prior knowledge, skills, and potential gaps or misconceptions, you can make informed decisions about how to tailor your teaching right from the start.

2. **Universally design with blended learning models (chapters 6, 7, and 8):** This phase emphasizes creating a universally

designed learning environment that strives to remove barriers, accommodate diverse learners, and promote active engagement. With the insights gained from the pre-assessment, you can design lessons using blended learning models, like the Station Rotation Model, to offer flexibility and accessibility for all students.

3. **Formative assessment (chapter 5):** Formative assessment data provides you with insight into student progress. As students engage with learning activities, you can monitor progress and identify areas where students may need additional support. This real-time data is crucial for adjusting instruction and ensuring that all students are moving toward firm, standards-aligned goals.

4. **Differentiated and personalized learning experiences (chapters 6, 7, and 8):** The data collected from formative assessments allows you to differentiate instruction effectively, adjusting the pace of instruction, offering different levels of support, or providing targeted interventions. This phase ensures that all students receive the appropriate challenges and support so that they can progress toward firm, standards-aligned learning objectives.

5. **Summative assessment (chapter 5):** Finally, the cycle culminates in summative assessments that evaluate student learning at the end of a unit or course. This data provides a snapshot of student achievement and feeds into the next cycle of instruction, helping you to refine your approach for future lessons.

Using this Data-Informed Design Cycle can help you create dynamic and responsive learning environments that are student centered. This approach not only supports the diverse needs of learners but also empowers teachers to be intentional and strategic in their instructional design. As we delve into each phase in detail, we'll explore practical strategies and real-world examples to help you implement each phase of the cycle effectively in your classroom.

## Summary

The Data-Informed Design Cycle provides a framework for creating differentiated, student-centered instruction. While blended learning opens the door to more flexible and engaging learning experiences, it's the strategic use of data that enables us to truly meet the diverse needs of our students. By leveraging a range of data—from pre-assessments to formative check-ins and summative evaluations—we can make more intentional decisions about how to design, adjust, and personalize instruction. The five interconnected phases of the cycle offer a clear process for making teaching more responsive and inclusive.

## Reflect and Discuss

1. How effectively are you currently using data to inform your instructional decisions, and where might there be room to grow?
2. In what ways do you see technology supporting your ability to collect and use data strategically to meet your students' individual needs?
3. What barriers do you face when trying to use data to design differentiated instruction, and how might the Data-Informed Design Cycle help you navigate those challenges?
4. Think about a recent lesson. How might you have changed your approach if you had used pre-assessment or formative data to guide the design?

> ## Time to Apply: Complete a Self-Assessment of Your Current Data Practices

**Objective:** Use the questions below to assess how you're currently using data to inform instruction and identify strategies that are already working.

### *Step 1: Self-Rating*

How often do you use data to guide your instructional decisions? Rate yourself on the scale below for each type of data.

| Data Source | Rarely | Occasionally | Consistently |
|---|---|---|---|
| Pre-assessment | | | |
| Formative assessment | | | |
| Data from online tools or platforms | | | |
| Summative assessment | | | |

### *Step 2: Reflection Questions*

Answer the questions below:

- Which data source(s) do you rely on most often, and why?
- What is one way you currently use data to differentiate instruction or provide support to learners?
- Where do you see opportunities to be more intentional with how you collect or use data in your classroom?
- What's one strategy you've used that's worked well to respond to student needs?

Keep these reflections in mind as you move through the next chapters—you'll gather ideas and strategies to deepen your data-informed design practice.

# CHAPTER 5

# Assessment

## Embracing My Role as Lead Learner: Using Data to Improve My Practice

When I first began implementing UDL and blended learning in my classroom, I wasn't just trying out new instructional models—I was engaging in a personal learning journey. I didn't know what I was doing at first, but I was determined to figure it out. In many ways, the pre-assessment phase of this journey was twofold: I immersed myself in books, research, and classroom examples to better understand how to design more inclusive and flexible learning experiences, and I gathered detailed input from my students. At the start of each year, I asked them to reflect on their strengths, challenges, interests, and learning preferences. This information became my starting point. It provided a foundation for designing lessons that would meet the needs of the unique group of students in each class.

As I began using blended learning models like the Station Rotation Model and the Playlist Model, I relied heavily on formative assessment to guide my day-to-day decisions. I watched how students moved through lessons, noted where they got stuck or disengaged, and used everything from exit tickets to informal student feedback to check the pulse of the class. I wasn't just assessing their learning—I was assessing my own design choices. What worked? What didn't? Which tools enhanced the experience, and which ones created barriers? I asked students to provide feedback along the way. Their feedback was invaluable.

At the end of each unit, I stepped back and looked at the bigger picture, essentially collecting critical summative assessment data. Were students mastering the key concepts and skills using these new instructional models? What did their performance and reflections tell me about how the blend of online and offline learning supported (or didn't support) their growth? I also collected end-of-unit feedback from students, asking which strategies helped them learn, what got in the way, and what they'd change for next time. Those reflections became the blueprint for how I would reimagine the unit moving forward.

As I struggled to shift my instructional practices, I embraced my role as the lead learner in the classroom. I had to be willing to experiment, fail, and adjust. Every piece of feedback, every observational note, and every student reflection helped me grow as a designer of learning experiences. And with each iteration, I got better at creating classrooms where all students could thrive.

## Firm Goals

By the end of this chapter, you will:

- Gain knowledge of best practices for using pre-assessment data to tailor your lessons to meet students' individual needs, addressing gaps or misconceptions.
- Understand the role of formative assessment in tracking student progress and informing ongoing adjustments to instruction and support.

- Know how to universally design summative assessments to evaluate overall student learning, measure mastery of key standards, and reflect on the effectiveness of your instructional approach.

## Pre-Assessment: Designing with Intention

Pre-assessment is the foundation of effective design because it allows you to meet students where they are, right from the start of a class or unit. Think of your classroom like a track with runners poised to begin their race: Each student is unique, starting from a different point based on their background and life experiences. To ensure every student can progress and succeed, you need to develop a clear understanding of where they are beginning in their learning journeys.

> *Pre-assessment is the foundation of effective design because it allows you to meet students where they are, right from the start.*

Pre-assessment data provides critical insight. It allows you to pinpoint what your students already know and identify the gaps or misconceptions in their understanding. Pre-assessment data allows you to design lessons and units that ensure each learner gets the support and challenges they need to stay engaged and develop their concept knowledge and skill sets. By tailoring your instruction, and differentiating learning experiences based on this initial data, you set the stage for maximizing learning outcomes for all students.

# Assessment

## *Pre-Assessment Strategies*

There are a variety of strategies you can use to collect pre-assessment data, as pictured in table 5.1.

**Table 5.1: Pre-Assessment Strategies**

| Pre-Assessment Strategies | |
|---|---|
| **Pre-test or quiz** | Before starting a new unit, give a pre-test or quiz to identify students' prior knowledge, skills, and understanding of upcoming content. |
| **Entrance or exit ticket** | Ask students to answer questions or complete an activity related to the upcoming lesson or unit. |
| **K-W-L chart (know, want to know, learned)** | Have students list what they know and want to learn about the topic before the lesson begins. |
| **Graphic organizers** | Provide students with a graphic organizer outlining the unit's fundamental concepts and ask them to complete it based on their knowledge of the topic. |
| **Self-assessment** | Ask students to assess their understanding of the content, skills, or learning objectives before a unit. |
| **Survey** | Administer a survey to students to gather information about their interests, prior knowledge, and learning preferences related to the topic. |
| **Sort-it-out concept map** | Give students a list of key terms or concepts related to the upcoming lesson or unit. Ask them to organize these terms into a concept map that connects these ideas and explains how they relate to one another. |
| **Anticipation guide** | Provide a list of statements related to the upcoming lesson and ask students to agree or disagree based on their prior knowledge. |
| **Quickwrite** | Ask students to write a short response to a question or prompt related to the upcoming lesson to gauge their understanding and prior knowledge. |
| **Two-minute talks or think-pair-share** | Ask students to think about a question or prompt, pair up with a classmate, and share their thoughts. |

If you're feeling daunted by the time needed to generate pre-assessments, AI can help! You can use AI tools to quickly generate standards-aligned pre-assessments tailored to your specific learning objectives. Start by inputting the standard or learning goal you're focused on into an AI-powered platform or chatbot. You can prompt the AI to create various types of questions—such as multiple-choice, short-answer, or even open-ended questions—that assess students' prior knowledge and readiness for the upcoming content.

Ideally, pre-assessments should always be standards-aligned and tailored to your specific learning objectives. Let's look at two examples of standards-aligned pre-assessments in tables 5.2 and 5.3.

**Table 5.2: Middle School Science Example: Standards-Aligned Pre-Assessment**

| Middle School Science Example: Standards-Aligned Pre-Assessment ||
|---|---|
| Imagine a middle school science teacher is about to teach a sequence of lessons focused on the Next Generation Science Standard (NGSS) MS-ESS2-4, the water cycle. The NGSS states that students must be able to "develop a model to describe the cycling of water through Earth's systems driven by energy from the sun and the force of gravity." ||
| **AI prompt** | Act as a curriculum designer and create a pre-assessment quiz with a mix of multiple-choice and short-answer questions on the water cycle and align them with NGSS MS-ESS2-4. |

## Assessment

| AI-generated pre-unit quiz questions | 1. Which of the following best describes the process of evaporation?<br>   A) Water vapor cools and turns into liquid water.<br>   B) Liquid water heats up and turns into water vapor.<br>   C) Water vapor forms clouds.<br>   D) Liquid water flows from rivers into the ocean.<br><br>2. Which force is primarily responsible for precipitation (rain, snow, etc.) falling to the ground?<br>   A) Wind<br>   B) Sunlight<br>   C) Gravity<br>   D) Temperature<br><br>3. Explain how the sun's energy drives the process of evaporation in the water cycle.<br><br>4. Describe the role of gravity in the water cycle. How does it influence where water moves in Earth's systems?<br><br>5. What happens during the process of condensation in the water cycle?<br>   A) Water vapor turns into liquid water.<br>   B) Water vapor escapes into space.<br>   C) Liquid water turns into water vapor.<br>   D) Ice turns directly into water vapor.<br><br>6. Draw and label a simple diagram of the water cycle. Include and label the processes of evaporation, condensation, precipitation, and runoff. |
|---|---|

Once students complete the quiz, review their answers to identify common misconceptions (e.g., confusion between evaporation and condensation or misunderstanding the role of gravity).

You can use this data to inform the design of your teacher-led station. For example, you might emphasize specific processes in upcoming lessons or provide instruction on background knowledge or pre-teaching vocabulary.

**Table 5.3: Elementary Math Example: Standards-Aligned Pre-Assessment**

| | *Elementary Math Example: Standards-Aligned Pre-Assessment* |
|---|---|
| | This pre-assessment is designed to gauge students' understanding of place value, specifically their ability to recognize the value of digits in three-digit numbers. The tasks will require students to demonstrate their ability to break down numbers and identify the value of each digit within a number. |
| **AI prompt** | Act as a curriculum designer and develop a set of tasks or problems that require students to demonstrate their understanding of place value and align it with CCSS.Math.Content.2.NBT.A.1. |
| **AI-generated pre-unit quiz questions** | Task 1: Identifying place value<br><br>• Write down the number 342.<br>• Ask students to:<br>• Circle the digit in the hundreds place and write its value<br>• Underline the digit in the tens place and write its value<br>• Box the digit in the ones place and write its value<br><br>Task 2: Breaking down the numbers<br><br>• Give students the number 576.<br>• Ask them to break down the number into hundreds, tens, and ones and write an equation showing the value of each digit.<br><br>Task 3: Comparing numbers<br><br>• Present two numbers: 483 and 528.<br>• Ask students to compare the two numbers and explain which number is greater and why.<br><br>Task 4: Place-value matching<br>• Provide a set of cards with different numbers (e.g., 645, 321, 784).<br>• Ask students to match each number with a corresponding description, such as:<br>  • This number has a 7 in the tens place.<br>  • This number has a 4 in the ones place.<br>  • This number has a 6 in the hundreds place. |

> Review students' responses to these tasks to assess their understanding of place value. Pay close attention to how students break down numbers and their ability to compare and create numbers based on place value.
>
> You can use this data to identify students who have a strong grasp of place value and those who may need additional support or practice with this fundamental concept. You can use this information to differentiate instruction at your teacher-led station, selecting number combinations at different levels of rigor and complexity. You can also incorporate specific supports and scaffolds to help students understand this process.

Since not all students enter a lesson with the same background knowledge or vocabulary, some will be ready to dive in, while others will need pre-teaching and support to access new learning. If we treat every student as if they're starting from the same place, we risk leaving some behind while alienating others. Students lacking the background knowledge or key vocabulary to access new information will feel frustrated and lost. By contrast, those with significant prior knowledge and vocabulary may become bored and disengage from the material since it feels repetitive and unnecessary.

This is where differentiating entry points becomes critical. Instead of delivering the same instruction to everyone, we must use what we have learned from pre-assessments to provide different learning pathways based on student needs, as pictured in table 5.4.

## The Station Rotation Model and UDL

### Table 5.4: Differentiate Entry Points Based on Pre-Assessment Data

| Pathway #1: Pre-Teaching Group | Pathway #2: Extension Group |
|---|---|
| **Vocabulary instruction:** Introduce key terms related to the lesson or content using images, diagrams, or real-world examples. Use the Frayer Model or a word wall to help students define the new vocabulary in their own words.<br><br>**Anchor new learning in prior knowledge:** Model how the new concept connects to something students may already know (e.g., "This is similar to . . .").<br><br>**Building background activity:** Provide students with instruction or resources to help them create a foundation of knowledge on which the instruction can build to ensure students can access the new information (e.g., video, text, explicit instruction, demonstration, modeling session).<br><br>**Hands-on exploration with manipulatives:** Provide interactive materials (e.g., number lines, maps, sentence strips, models) and let students physically engage with the concept. | **Inquiry and research extension:** Invite students to research a high-interest question related to the topic or present them with a real-world application to explore (e.g., find a real-world example of [concept] in action and explain how it works).<br><br>**Create a model or analogy:** Ask students to explain a concept by creating a model, drawing, or analogy (e.g., create a visual or analogy to show how this concept works).<br><br>**Debate or defend a position:** Provide students with a series of statements related to the content of the lesson or lessons and ask them to engage in a discussion with a group about their position on each. Or you can provide them another pathway to present their position (e.g., drawing, concept map, writing).<br><br>**Reciprocal teaching strategy with media:** Give a group time to read an article or listen to a podcast on a related, high-interest topic and use the reciprocal teaching protocol to discuss it in depth. |

Differentiating entry points based on prior knowledge allows teachers to provide the right level of support or challenge, keeping every student engaged in rigorous, purposeful learning instead of allowing them to feel lost or unchallenged.

## Formative Assessment: Tracking Progress Toward Learning Objectives

In any classroom, students progress at different rates. Some grasp new concepts and skills quickly, while others may require additional support, feedback, or reteaching to fully understand and apply their learning. Formative assessment is the process of gathering information about students' understanding as they progress toward firm, standards-aligned learning goals. Unlike summative assessment, which occurs at the end of a unit, formative assessment is ongoing, embedded, and informal. It's designed to help you to identify where differentiation, additional scaffolds, targeted support, or extension activities might be needed.

To accurately identify each individual student's needs, it's best practice to collect formative assessment data in each lesson—not just to measure progress toward individual learning objectives but to ensure that students are on track to meet the larger goals of the unit.

Formative assessment can take many forms, from quick checks for understanding to more structured activities that capture students' progress. The key is to integrate these assessments into your lessons seamlessly, which allows you to adjust your teaching strategies based on the data you collect. This may involve using technology tools to capture a quick snapshot of where students are—especially if you're facilitating a teacher-led station and need to review the data later.

Collecting formative assessment data enables you to do the following:

- **Adjust instruction:** Formative assessments help you gauge how effective your instruction has been in helping students understand concepts and apply skills. If a significant number of students are struggling, it may be necessary to modify your approach or provide additional support.

- **Address misconceptions:** Formative assessments allow you to identify misconceptions or gaps in understanding early so you can address them before they become larger obstacles to learning course content.
- **Support student reflection:** Sharing formative assessment data with students empowers them to set goals, monitor their progress, and reflect on their learning. This reflective practice fosters a deeper awareness of their strengths and limitations but also encourages them to take an active role in their learning.

By embedding regular, informal assessments into your lessons, you create a dynamic and responsive learning experience where instruction is continually informed by student data. This approach ensures that every student is supported as they progress toward learning objectives, which helps them build the knowledge and skills they need to succeed in both the immediate lesson and the broader unit.

---

*By embedding regular, informal assessments into your lessons, you create a dynamic and responsive learning experience where instruction is continually informed by student data.*

---

# Formative Assessment Strategies

There are different categories of formative assessment, including observational assessments, checks for understanding, and formative feedback.

## *Make Observational Assessments*

Your observations of student behaviors, interactions, and work provide valuable qualitative data (information that is descriptive and non-numeric) that complements quantitative assessments like quizzes, which produce numerical data. Qualitative assessment techniques such as checklists, observational rubrics, and rating scales thus allow you to gain insights into students' progress, engagement, and learning strategies.

**1. Observations with a checklist:** Simply observing our students at work can provide valuable insights into their behaviors, interactions, and level of understanding during classroom activities.

You can use observations with a checklist when students are:

- Engaged in group activities or discussions (to monitor individual participation and contributions)
- Working independently or in pairs (to assess their engagement, problem-solving strategies, and use of resources)
- Completing hands-on tasks or projects (to evaluate their skills, collaboration, and attention to task requirements)

You might include the following items on a checklist:

- **Participation:** Is the student actively engaged in the activity/discussion?
- **Contribution:** Does the student contribute relevant ideas, questions, or solutions?
- **Collaboration:** How effectively does the student work with peers, share responsibilities, and communicate?

- **Problem-solving**: Can students apply critical thinking and problem-solving strategies to overcome challenges?
- **Use of resources:** Is the student effectively utilizing available resources (e.g., materials, peers, technology, references)?
- **Task completion:** To what extent does the student complete tasks within the given time frame?
- **Understanding:** Does the student clearly understand concepts, instructions, and learning objectives?

**2. Observation paired with a simple rubric:** You can assess students' performance or behavior during a learning activity with a simple standards-aligned, four-point mastery scale rubric using asset-based language. This helps you develop a strategy for providing students with clear feedback on their strengths as well as areas where they can grow and improve.

For example, imagine small groups of students using the reciprocal teaching strategy to unpack a text or discuss a video. You could observe students and circle language on an asset-based rubric, like the one pictured in table 5.5, to informally assess their participation in the process or their understanding of how to apply the comprehension strategies. At the end of the discussion, you could distribute the rubrics and then ask students to review their assessment as a way to reflect on what they learned.

## Table 5.5: Four-Point Asset-Based Reciprocal Teaching Rubric

| Criteria | Beginning 1 | Developing 2 | Proficient 3 | Mastery 4 |
|---|---|---|---|---|
| **Engagement in the process** | The student is starting to observe group discussions and shows potential to contribute more actively. They may focus on listening and are beginning to recognize the value of peer interaction. | The student shows growing engagement by sharing ideas or responses, especially with prompting or encouragement. They are learning to participate and are beginning to take more initiative in discussions. | The student actively participates in discussions, sharing ideas, listening attentively, and responding meaningfully to peers. They demonstrate consistent engagement and contribute to the success of the group. | The student leads and enhances group discussions by asking thought-provoking questions, guiding others, and deepening the group's understanding. Their participation is thoughtful and supports group success. |
| **Use of comprehension strategies** | The student is beginning to explore comprehension strategies (predicting, questioning, clarifying, summarizing) with support. They are building confidence in applying these strategies. | The student demonstrates a growing use of comprehension strategies, applying them with support or prompting. Their ability to use strategies is developing and becoming more consistent over time. | The student effectively applies comprehension strategies independently and consistently. They use these strategies to deepen group understanding and contribute meaningfully to the process. | The student confidently applies comprehension strategies and supports others in using them effectively. They connect strategies to deeper insights, concepts, or themes, helping elevate the group's understanding. |

## Check for Understanding

Techniques for checking understanding, as pictured in table 5.6, are quick, targeted assessments that help determine whether students grasp the key concepts of a lesson. Such assessments can include asking students to summarize what they've learned, using exit tickets, or employing technology-based tools like quick polls or quizzes.

**Table 5.6: Formative Assessment Strategies**

| Check for Understanding Strategies | |
|---|---|
| **Quick polls** | Integrate quick polls into your lessons to collect data from students. You can use polls to gauge understanding, identify misconceptions or gaps, and check in with students. |
| **Tell me how** | Instead of relying solely on written explanations to assess what students know or can do, let students communicate verbally on video. "Tell me how" gives students who excel at verbally articulating their thoughts the chance to surface their learning.<br><br>Ask students to record a video:<br><br>• Explaining how they solved a problem<br>• Describing the strategies they used to complete a task<br>• Summarizing the main ideas from a chapter in a textbook<br>• Making predictions about what they expect to happen in a lab or a novel<br>• Identifying a new vocabulary word and explaining it to their peers<br>• Reflecting on what they understand as well as what is confusing or unclear about a topic, text, or task |
| **Create an analogy** | Ask students to make a comparison or create an analogy. Comparison challenges students to think critically about a thing's qualities or characteristics. |

| **Error analysis** | Generate a series of problems, or a sample of work, that contains errors. Ask students to find the mistakes, correct them, and explain (in writing or verbally in a video recording) how they knew the errors were present. Then, task them with explaining how they went about fixing them. |
|---|---|
| **Quick quiz** | Create a quick assessment to determine what students understand or can do. Consider asking questions about:<br><br>• Key concepts or ideas<br>• Vocabulary<br>• Specific skills<br>• Formulas or processes |
| **Write a summary** | Challenge students to identify the main ideas in a lesson, video, article, chapter, or podcast and write a summary identifying and describing those key ideas or main points. |
| **Draw a concept map or flowchart** | Ask students to surface their learning visually.<br><br>Encourage them to begin by identifying the main concepts covered in a lesson, video, article, chapter, or podcast. Then have them create a concept map or flowchart to show how those concepts fit together. |
| **Rate your understanding** | Ask students to evaluate their understanding of key concepts, processes, formulas, vocabulary, or skills. Teachers of younger learners can use an emoji scale like the ones available in Pear Deck. Teachers of older learners may want to create their "rate your understanding" activity inside a digital form and ask students to explain why they gave themselves a particular rating. |
| **3-2-1** | Gather quick formative assessment data by asking students to complete a 3-2-1 activity:<br><br>• What are three things they learned?<br>• What two questions do they have?<br>• What is one thing they would like more help with or are confused about? |

Let's look at two examples of standards-aligned formative assessments in tables 5.7 and 5.8. Again, you might rely on AI tools to help you generate assessments, or you can create your own.

**Table 5.7: Elementary Example: English Language Arts (ELA)**

| *Elementary Example: English Language Arts (ELA)* | |
|---|---|
| **Third grade** | Determine the main idea of a text, recount the key details, and explain how they support the main idea (aligned with CCSS.ELA-Literacy.RI.3.2). |
| **Observational checklist for group work** | As students work in small groups at the teacher-led station to read a short informational text, the teacher uses an observational checklist to monitor students' ability to identify the main idea and supporting details. The checklist includes criteria such as:<br><br>• Identifies the main idea of the text<br>• Accurately selects key details that support the main idea<br>• Participates in group discussions by sharing relevant ideas<br>• Uses text evidence to support their points |
| By observing students as they work through the text, you can gather real-time data on their comprehension skills. This data will help determine if additional instruction or scaffolding is needed or if the group is ready to move on to more complex texts. The observational checklist also provides insights into students' collaboration skills, helping to inform future group assignments. | |

Table 5.8: Secondary Example: Social Studies

*Secondary Example: History*

| Tenth grade | Analyze primary and secondary sources (aligned with CCSS.ELA-Literacy.RH.9-10.9). Compare and contrast treatments of the same topic in several primary and secondary sources. |
|---|---|
| "Tell me how" video explanation | In this activity, students will either record a short video (30 to 60 seconds) or write an explanation detailing the complex causes of World War I. This strategy not only assesses their understanding of the material but also provides an opportunity for students who excel at verbal or written communication to demonstrate their learning. |
| Example prompts for the video | Use your analysis of and evidence from the primary and secondary sources to:<br><br>• Explain how a specific alliance system contributed to the outbreak of World War I.<br>• Describe the role of militarism and how it escalated tensions among European powers.<br>• Summarize how nationalism influenced the actions of key countries leading up to the war.<br>• Reflect on which cause of World War I was most significant and why. |
| | These quick video recordings or written paragraphs will allow the teacher to assess students' understanding of the multiple and often interconnected causes of World War I. By listening to how students articulate their thoughts, the teacher can identify any misconceptions or gaps in understanding. This data will inform the next steps in instruction. |

Formative assessment data is more than just a snapshot of where students are in their progress toward firm, standards-aligned learning goals. It is a powerful tool teachers can use to identify needs and differentiate instruction effectively. The true value of formative assessment lies in its ability to inform these instructional decisions, allowing you to tailor your teaching to meet the unique needs of each student.

# Summative Assessment: Measuring Mastery with Multiple Means of Action and Expression

Summative assessment provides a culminating snapshot of student learning at the end of a unit, project, or instructional cycle. Its primary purpose is to evaluate the extent to which students have mastered key concepts and skills aligned to the learning objectives and standards. Whereas formative assessment offers information to guide instruction along the way, summative assessment helps you and your students reflect on the effectiveness of the learning journey.

To ensure summative assessments are meaningful and equitable, it's critical to align them closely with your unit's desired results—the specific concepts, skills, and competencies students should be able to demonstrate by the end of a learning cycle. When assessments are misaligned or narrowly defined, they may fail to capture what students actually know and can do.

Too often, summative assessments take a single form—like a written test or essay—that all students are expected to complete in the same way. This approach can create barriers for students with different strengths, language proficiencies, or learning needs. A student who fully understands a concept may struggle to express it through a written response not because they lack understanding, but because the format doesn't align with how they communicate best. If we want an accurate picture of student learning, we need to provide flexible assessment pathways that allow students to choose the mode of expression that enables them to demonstrate their knowledge most effectively.

*If we want an accurate picture of student learning, we need to provide flexible assessment pathways that allow students to choose the mode of expression that enables them to demonstrate their knowledge most effectively.*

This is where UDL can elevate summative assessment. By offering multiple means of action and expression, you empower students to choose how they demonstrate their learning in a way that reflects their strengths. Instead of a one-size-fits-all test, you can provide a choice board of summative options: a traditional assessment, a visual or multimedia presentation, a written explanation, a performance task, or a creative product like a video, podcast, or comic strip. What matters most is that each option is construct specific and designed to assess the same core learning outcomes, as shown in the examples in tables 5.9 and 5.10.

**Table 5.9: Elementary Summative Assessment Example: Math**

| Elementary Summative Assessment: Math | |
|---|---|
| **Fourth grade** | Understand a fraction a/b with a >1 as a sum of fractions 1/b. Decompose a fraction into a sum of fractions with the same denominator in more than one way (aligned with CCSS.Math.Content.4.NF.B.3). |
| **Assessment option 1** | **Create a comic strip:** Draw a comic that shows a real-life scenario involving decomposing a fraction (e.g., sharing a pizza or chocolate bar). Include at least two different ways to break apart the same fraction and explain how your character solves the problem. |
| **Assessment option 2** | **Teach the concept in a video or slideshow:** Record a short video or create a visual presentation where you teach someone how to decompose fractions in more than one way. Include at least two examples and explain your thinking step by step. |

Table 5.10: Secondary Summative Assessment Example: English

## Secondary Summative Assessment: English

| | |
|---|---|
| Ninth to tenth grade | Analyze how complex characters (e.g., those with multiple or conflicting motivations) develop over the course of a text, interact with other characters, and advance the plot or develop the theme (aligned with CCSS.ELA-Literacy.RL.9-10.3). |
| Assessment option 1 | **Write a literary analysis essay:** Craft a formal essay that analyzes how a character changes throughout the story, how their motivations affect the plot, and how their relationships contribute to the theme. Include textual evidence to support your ideas. |
| Assessment option 2 | **Design a character timeline and reflection:** Create a visual timeline that traces key moments in a character's development. Annotate each moment with insights about their motivations, relationships, and impact on the theme supported by evidence from the text. Include a short written or recorded reflection explaining your analysis. |

Universally designed summative assessments not only provide a more accurate picture of student achievement, but they also promote agency and engagement. When students have voice and choice in how they show what they've learned, they are more likely to take ownership of the process—and the product. Whether students are writing an analytical essay, building a model, recording a screencast, or leading a demonstration, each path offers an opportunity to make learning visible in meaningful ways.

It's natural for teachers to wonder how to fairly assess different types of student products, like a written essay versus a visual timeline, or a comic strip versus a video explanation. The key is to remember that we're not assessing the format of the product; we're assessing the construct—the specific concept, skill, or learning outcome students are being asked to demonstrate. For example, tables 5.11 and 5.12 show standards-aligned, asset-based rubrics that an elementary math teacher or a secondary English teacher can use to assess whatever option a student may choose to demonstrate their learning.

## Assessment

**Table 5.11: Elementary Math Assessment: Standards-Aligned, Asset-Based Rubric**

| Criteria | Beginning 1 | Developing 2 | Proficient 3 | Mastery 4 |
|---|---|---|---|---|
| **Fraction decomposition** | The student works on representing fractions as sums, beginning to apply decomposition strategies. | The student shows progress in decomposing fractions using one or more approaches. | The student accurately decomposes fractions using more than one method. | The student clearly and accurately decomposes multiple fractions using a variety of methods and explains each one in detail. |
| **Conceptual understanding** | The student builds understanding of parts and wholes in fractions. | The student demonstrates developing understanding of how fractions can be decomposed. | The student shows solid understanding of how fraction parts relate and can be combined. | The student demonstrates deep conceptual understanding of fraction equivalence and the relationship between parts and wholes. |
| **Clarity of communication** | The student begins to express ideas, working on using mathematical vocabulary. | The student communicates ideas with growing use of math vocabulary and visuals. | The student communicates thinking clearly using appropriate vocabulary and explanations. | The student communicates reasoning clearly and confidently using precise vocabulary and visuals to enhance understanding. |

**Table 5.12: Secondary English Assessment: Standards-Aligned, Asset-Based Rubric**

| Criteria | Beginning 1 | Developing 2 | Proficient 3 | Mastery 4 |
|---|---|---|---|---|
| **Character analysis** | The student shares basic observations about the character's actions or traits. | The student identifies key aspects of the character and begins to explore development or motivation. | The student explains how the character changes and contributes to the plot or theme. | The student offers thoughtful insights into the character's complexity, motivations, and connections to larger ideas in the text. |
| **Use of textual evidence** | The student uses selected text references to support initial ideas. | The student includes relevant examples or quotes to begin supporting analysis. | The student uses specific and well-chosen evidence to support claims. | The student seamlessly integrates precise, relevant evidence to strengthen and deepen the analysis. |
| **Connection to plot or theme** | The student begins to recognize the character's impact on the story. | The student explores how the character contributes to plot events or themes. | The student makes clear connections between the character's actions and key elements of plot or theme. | The student demonstrates insightful connections that reveal how the character drives both plot and deeper thematic meaning. |

When summative assessment options are construct specific, meaning they all ask students to show evidence of the same standard or learning goal, you can confidently use a single, standards-aligned, asset-based rubric to assess all submissions. For example, if the goal is to analyze how a character develops across a text, both a formal essay and a visual timeline can be assessed using the same criteria: depth of analysis, use of textual evidence, and understanding of how the character advances the plot or theme.

In addition to evaluating student learning, summative assessments can also help you reflect on your instructional design. When viewed collectively, the data from summative assessments reveals which strategies and scaffolds supported student success—and where gaps remain. Combined with student feedback about the unit or project, these insights can help you refine future instruction and strengthen alignment between your learning goals, instructional strategies, and assessment practices.

## Summary

Designing with data allows you to bring a high level of intentionality to your planning, moving away from teaching to the mythical middle and instead designing for the diverse learners in your room. By using pre-assessment data, you can gain a clear understanding of what your students already know or can do at the start of a unit, and you can identify any gaps or misconceptions that need to be addressed. As students progress, formative assessment helps you track individual growth toward learning objectives so you can adjust your instruction, differentiate support, and ensure no one falls through the cracks. This responsive approach keeps all students engaged and moving steadily toward firm, standards-aligned goals. Summative assessment then gives students a culminating opportunity to show what they've learned. When you offer multiple pathways for students to express their understanding or skills, you're more likely to capture an accurate, equitable picture of their progress.

## Reflect and Discuss

1. How often do you collect and use pre-assessment data prior to designing lessons and units? Which of the pre-assessment strategies presented in this chapter are most appealing to you?

2. What formative assessment strategies do you find most effective in your classroom? How could technology enhance your ability to collect and analyze formative assessment data during and after lessons?

3. Think about a recent lesson where you used formative assessment data to differentiate instruction. How did you adjust your teaching to meet the needs of different learners? What strategies do you currently use to differentiate instruction, and where do you see opportunities for growth (e.g., content, process, product, learning environment)?

4. How might leveraging AI tools help you generate standards-aligned assessments and make this a more sustainable part of your teaching practice?

5. How would data-informed design help you to make the lessons and learning experiences in your classroom more accessible, inclusive, and equitable? How would this impact the learners and the culture in your classroom?

## Time to Apply: Design a Data-Informed Differentiated Lesson

**Objective:** Use your favorite AI-powered education tool or chatbot to develop an informal assessment strategy that will help you differentiate effectively based on data.

## Step 1: Select or Create a Lesson

First, you'll need to choose a lesson to customize with your assessment strategy:

- Select a lesson you've previously used, or use an AI-powered tool or chatbot to create a new one focused on a specific standard or learning objective.
- Identify what you want students to learn, and think about past challenges you've faced when teaching this topic, concept, or skill.

## Step 2: Develop a Pre-Assessment Strategy

Next, you'll need to decide what strategy to apply to your lesson:

- Select a pre-assessment strategy from this chapter, or use AI to generate pre-assessment questions or activities that will help you understand what your students already know about the topic, concept, or skill and identify their gaps or misconceptions.
- Align the pre-assessment to specific standards or learning objectives to ensure it provides you with actionable data to guide your design.

## Step 3: Add "Check for Understanding" Formative Assessment

Select a strategy from this chapter to check for understanding, and use an AI-powered tool or chatbot to ensure it is aligned with standards. Add it to your lesson to assess student progress toward a learning objective.

## Step 4: Analyze Assessment Data

Think about what you would look for in the data. How will you identify student needs?

## Step 5: Seek Peer Feedback

Find a colleague to provide you with feedback on your assessment strategies. Are there any adjustments or modifications they suggest? Use the feedback you receive to edit and refine your lesson.

**CHAPTER 6**

# The Teacher-Led Station and Differentiation

## Planning the Perfect Day at Disneyland: A Lesson in Differentiation

Two years ago, I planned a family trip to Disneyland in Los Angeles to celebrate my daughter's sixteenth birthday. Our group was wonderfully diverse: my two teenagers, my pregnant sister and her husband, and their two-year-old son. The challenge was clear. How could we ensure that everyone, from the excited teens to the curious toddler, enjoyed their Disneyland experience without dragging the entire group around the park all day?

As soon as we arrived, it was immediately apparent that a one-size-fits-all approach wouldn't work. My teenagers were eager to rush to the thrill rides like Space Mountain and Indiana Jones Adventure. Meanwhile, my two-year-old nephew was captivated by the ducks wandering Main Street and the enchanting world of Fantasyland, where he could meet his favorite characters and enjoy rides like Dumbo the Flying Elephant.

To make the most of our day, we decided to split up strategically. My sister and her husband took charge of their toddler, heading straight to Fantasyland. They planned their morning around character meet-and-greets and a scheduled break at one of the shaded areas to let their son rest, enjoy snacks, and avoid a meltdown from hunger or overstimulation.

Meanwhile, I took my teenagers to Tomorrowland to start our day with some high-speed rides. We mapped out a plan to hit all the big rides they were excited about, allowing them the freedom to explore while ensuring we had meeting points and times to regroup.

After the morning excitement, we all met up for lunch, sharing our experiences and enjoying some downtime together.

In the afternoon, we switched things up. My sister's husband, who enjoys a good roller coaster, took the teenagers on some of the more adventurous rides they had missed earlier, while I spent some time with my sister and nephew in Toontown.

By the evening, we reconvened to watch the parade and fireworks together—a magical end to our day. Each member of our group had the chance to enjoy Disneyland in a way that suited their interests, age, and energy levels.

This experience highlighted the importance of differentiation—tailoring our plans to meet the different needs of everyone in the group. By allowing each person to have a unique and personalized experience, we ensured that the day was enjoyable and memorable for all.

In much the same way that we tailored our day at Disneyland to ensure each family member had a magical day, differentiating instruction in the classroom is about designing learning experiences that strive to meet the needs of your students' varied abilities, interests, and readiness levels.

The teacher-led station in a rotation model allows for targeted instruction, modeling, and support. Facilitating small-group instruction at the teacher-led station allows teachers to differentiate content or processes to meet students where they are, ensuring each one has access to learning experiences that challenge them within their zone of proximal development.[1]

Just as our day at Disneyland was enjoyable and successful because we met everyone's unique needs, a well-designed teacher-led station ensures that all students can engage meaningfully and progress in their individual learning journey.

## Firm Goals

By the end of this chapter, you will:

- Grasp the importance of differentiation and the four key areas where differentiation can be most impactful.
- See how to differentiate effectively at your teacher-led station to provide strong Tier 1 instruction for all students.
- Understand how to structure and design your teacher-led station using a collection of instructional strategies that can be used to differentiate instruction and engage students.
- Know how to differentiate for both skill-level and mixed-skill-level groupings at the teacher-led station.

## Differentiation: Responding to Student Needs

Differentiation involves tailoring your curriculum, instructional strategies, resources, and learning activities to meet the diverse needs of individual students and small groups within the classroom. By adjusting these elements, you ensure that all students can engage with course material in ways that align with their unique abilities and learning preferences. This fosters an environment where every student can succeed regardless of their starting point.

Differentiation is the natural next step in the process of data-informed teaching. Differentiation, as defined by Carol Ann Tomlinson, an expert of differentiated instruction, is the practice of adapting instruction to meet students' various needs. In an ASCD publication, Tomlinson expands on this idea:

> Differentiating instruction means that the teacher anticipates the differences in the students' readiness, interests, and learning profiles and, as a result, creates different learning paths so that students have the opportunity to learn as much as they can as deeply as they can, without undue anxiety because the assignments are too taxing—or boredom because they are not challenging enough.[2]

To design learning paths that align with students' readiness, interests, and learning preferences, teachers must first collect and analyze data—both before and during instruction. Pre-assessment and formative assessment are essential tools that allow us to respond to learner variability in meaningful, intentional ways. Differentiation allows you to take the insights gained from pre-assessments and formative assessments and use them to design learning experiences that are responsive to each student's progress, skills, and abilities. Whether this recalibration means adjusting the pace of instruction, providing alternative resources, or offering varied ways for students to engage with the material and demonstrate their understanding, differentiation ensures that every student has the opportunity to succeed.

Differentiation recognizes that students come to class with varying levels of background knowledge, skills, and interests. Rather than provide a one-size-fits-all experience, teachers who differentiate offer multiple pathways for students to achieve the same learning goals. This customization is much easier to accomplish in a blended learning environment where students are not asked to move in lockstep through a single lesson or learning experience.

Tomlinson emphasizes that differentiation is a responsive and proactive approach to teaching designed to address the diverse needs of students within the same classroom, ensuring that every student is challenged and supported according to their individual readiness.[3]

Further, Tomlinson explains teachers can focus on differentiating four key elements:

- **Content:** Teachers differentiate content by providing materials at varying levels of difficulty or by offering different types of resources, such as texts, videos, or hands-on activities. For example, some teachers assign spelling lists or vocabulary based on pre-assessment results, ensuring that each student works on words that are appropriately challenging for their current level.
- **Process:** Teachers differentiate process by adjusting how they ask students to make sense of the content, offering multiple options and various scaffolds to support them, like graphic organizers. For example, students might work on tasks at varying levels of complexity but all focused on the same learning goal. They may have access to sentence stems or deconstructed examples.
- **Product:** Teachers can differentiate products by allowing students to demonstrate their understanding in various ways. Teachers might offer students multiple options for their final projects, encouraging them to choose formats that align with their interests, such as creating a video, writing an essay, or developing a creative presentation. The products students work on may also have different levels of rigor.

- **Learning environment:** Differentiation also extends to the classroom environment, where teachers create spaces that are flexible and supportive of all learners. There may be spaces designated for individual learning tasks and others designed to support collaborative tasks.

Table 6.1 shows how teachers may differentiate these four elements of their students' learning experience.

**Table 6.1: Classroom Elements to Differentiate Paired with Examples**

| Element | Examples | In a Blended Learning Environment |
|---|---|---|
| **Content** | Provide reading materials at varying levels of difficulty.<br><br>Offer video lectures, podcasts, or infographics on the same topic. Let students choose based on their preferences.<br><br>Offer small-group instruction, presenting information at a level that is accessible. | Assign different online articles or digital resources based on students' reading levels using platforms like Newsela or AI text levelers. Allow students to read independently or with a partner.<br><br>Use the teacher-led station to provide differentiated instruction.<br><br>Curate multimedia resources for students to explore. |

| | | |
|---|---|---|
| **Process** | Offer varied graphic organizers to help students organize their thoughts (e.g., mind maps, outlines).<br><br>Assign tiered activities where all students work on the same essential skills but at different levels of complexity.<br><br>Provide different options for meaning-making that appeal to students who may want to work individually (e.g., reflective summary) or collaboratively (e.g., small-group discussion). | Use online discussions where students can engage in peer-to-peer learning at their own pace.<br><br>Create interactive online modules that students can complete at their own pace, with scaffolds and support as needed.<br><br>Use adaptive learning platforms that adjust content difficulty based on student responses (e.g., Khan Academy). |
| **Product** | Allow students to choose how they demonstrate their understanding (e.g., essay, video presentation, artistic representation).<br><br>Use asset-based rubrics that outline different expectations for different levels of proficiency.<br><br>Offer a choice board or "menu" of project options, catering to different interests, strengths, and preferences. | Have students create digital portfolios using platforms like Seesaw or Google Sites to demonstrate their learning over time.<br><br>Use multimedia tools like Canva or QuickTime to create videos, posters, or digital presentations as final products.<br><br>Encourage students to produce podcasts or publish blogs on the subject matter. |

| | | |
|---|---|---|
| **Learning environment** | Provide flexible seating arrangements to accommodate different learning preferences.<br><br>Create quiet zones and collaboration zones within the classroom.<br><br>Incorporate various materials and resources that reflect different cultures and perspectives. | Use a rotation model where students move between different learning stations, both online and offline, tailored to their needs.<br><br>Create virtual learning spaces in an LMS where students can access resources, participate in discussions, and collaborate on projects at their own pace. |

In a differentiated classroom, the teacher continuously assesses students' progress, identifying their learning needs and creatively adjusting their instruction to provide the best possible support.

Differentiation requires teachers to use time flexibly, employ various instructional strategies, and collaborate with students to shape the learning experience. Tomlinson emphasizes that differentiation is about providing specific alternatives that allow each student to learn as deeply and as quickly as possible without assuming that one student's learning path will look identical to another's. Creating flexible pathways is critical to ensuring all students are appropriately supported and challenged in the learning environment.

The Station Rotation Model is ideal for differentiation because it creates the structure and flexibility teachers need to respond to the diverse needs of students. By breaking the class into smaller groups and rotating them through a series of learning activities, teachers can design multiple entry points, scaffolded tasks, and targeted supports.

The model allows for variation in how students access information (e.g., multimedia or text), engage in meaning-making (e.g., collaborative discussion or independent practice), and demonstrate understanding (e.g., creative products or written reflections). This flexibility enables teachers to use time more intentionally, design activities that honor learner variability, and increase student agency. Rather than expect all students to learn the same way, at the same time, and at the same pace, the Station Rotation Model supports multiple pathways toward shared learning goals.

> *Rather than expect all students to learn the same way, at the same time, and at the same pace, the Station Rotation Model supports multiple pathways toward shared learning goals.*

While differentiation can and should occur across all stations, the teacher-led station is often the best place to begin. For educators new to the Station Rotation Model, differentiating at the teacher-led station feels both manageable and impactful. This is where teachers can work with a small number of students at a time, use pre-assessment or formative data to group students by need, and customize instruction in real time. Whether it's offering extra scaffolding, modeling a strategy, or extending the learning for students who are ready for more, the teacher can provide responsive, targeted support that isn't possible in a whole-group setting. This focused attention not only helps close gaps but also builds stronger teacher-student relationships and creates more equitable access to instruction.

## Small-Group Differentiated Instructional Strategies

In this section, we'll explore five different instructional strategies you can use to structure your time with students and more effectively differentiate the teacher-led station. Remember, when designing the teacher-led station, it is important to use pre-assessment or diagnostic data to identify the various skill levels or needs in a class, as discussed in chapter 5. That data can help you to design the teacher-led station in ways that ensure the appropriate level of rigor and complexity and prepare the necessary scaffolds.

When transitioning from whole-group to small-group instruction, it's important to resist the urge to replicate the whole-group experience at a smaller scale. Simply repeating the same mini-lesson for each group not only results in lost time and teacher fatigue, but it also misses the opportunity to tailor instruction to students' specific needs. If we want to differentiate meaningfully, the small-group experience must be more interactive, targeted, and responsive—it should not be a series of identical explanations delivered on repeat.

For many teachers, moving away from familiar lecture-style teaching can feel daunting. That's why this chapter offers a set of practical strategies to help you structure the teacher-led station in ways that engage learners actively, address diverse skill levels, and make differentiation both manageable and impactful.

It's important to note that differentiation can happen when you group students by skill or ability level, but you can also differentiate when working with mixed-skill-level groups, as pictured in table 6.2. In a mixed-skill-level group, you can strategically pair students for support, provide texts, prompts, problems, and tasks at different levels of rigor and complexity, and provide additional scaffolding, support, and feedback for individual students in a small teacher-led group.

### Table 6.2: Skill-Level vs. Mixed-Skill-Level Groupings at the Teacher-Led Station

| Skill-Level Grouping | Mixed-Skill-Level Grouping |
|---|---|
| **Group composition:** Students are grouped by their current skill level (e.g., advanced, proficient, emerging). This allows you to target instruction to each group's specific needs and readiness. | **Group composition:** Students are grouped with a mix of abilities. This promotes peer-to-peer interaction, allowing stronger students to support and mentor others while reinforcing their understanding. |
| **Instructional focus:** You can scaffold or extend learning based on each group's proficiency level. For example, advanced students may tackle more complex problems or higher-order thinking tasks, while emerging students receive more foundational support. | **Instructional focus:** You provide differentiated support for students at various levels within the same instructional session. The goal is to facilitate discussion and peer teaching, providing multiple entry points to the content. |
| **UDL principle in action:** Use "multiple means of representation" by providing accessible content tailored to the group's ability. For instance, for emerging readers, the teacher might use simpler text or read aloud, while more advanced students might analyze a more complex text. | **UDL principle in action:** Use "multiple means of engagement" by fostering collaboration and communication between students. In a mixed-ability group, diverse perspectives and approaches to solving problems are encouraged, supporting all learners. |
| **Elementary math example:** In a skill-level group, you might focus on foundational multiplication skills with one group while challenging another group to solve multi-step word problems involving multiplication and division. | **Middle school science example:** In a mixed-skill group, model the process of reading and interpreting data from a line graph. When students transition to pair practice, provide graphs at varying levels of rigor and complexity. More advanced pairs of students receive graphs with multiple data sets and variables to analyze, while students needing more support work with simpler graphs that focus on one variable, receiving guiding questions to aid their analysis. |

Each teacher-led instructional strategy described below can be used with skill-level or mixed-skill-level groupings.

As you design differentiated stations, think beyond simply delivering content. The goal is not to dominate the station with extended teacher talk but to create a dynamic learning environment where students become active participants in the learning process.

Using clear structures to organize the teacher-led station positions students to take ownership of the process, transforming the station into a space where they are encouraged to think critically, engage in creative problem-solving, communicate with their peers, and collaborate on shared tasks. By structuring the station with intentional strategies, teachers can foster student engagement and ensure every learner is actively involved in meaningful work. The five strategies below are designed to do just that!

## Teacher-Led Instructional Strategy #1: "I Do, We Do, Pairs Do, You Do"

The "I do, we do, pairs do, you do" instructional strategy is designed to provide explicit instruction, scaffold student learning, and gradually release responsibility from teacher to student. The goal is to support students as they move from explicit instruction and modeling to practicing skills independently, ensuring they build confidence and competence along the way. How does the "I do, we do, pairs do, you do" strategy work?

## Step 1: I Do

Model the skill or concept. This stage involves explicit instruction: You demonstrate how to approach a problem, complete a task, or understand a concept. Describe your process explicitly as a think-aloud so students can understand the cognitive processes involved.

## Step 2: We Do

Work together on the task. During this step, provide guided practice, engaging students in the process while offering support and feedback. This collaborative practice helps students gain confidence as they attempt to implement the skill or understand the concept.

## Step 3: Pairs Do

Students work in pairs to practice the skill or concept. This stage encourages peer learning and collaboration, allowing students to discuss their thinking, share strategies, and support each other. Monitor each pair's progress, identifying students who may need additional instruction and support.

## Step 4: You Do

Students ready to transition to independent work continue to apply the skill or concept. In this final phase, students demonstrate their understanding and ability to complete the task independently. At the same time, you can continue to work with students who struggled with the "pairs do" activity, providing additional instruction, walking through another model, or making scaffolds available.

The "I do, we do, pairs do, you do" strategy is far more effective in small groups because it allows you to closely monitor each student's progress as responsibility is gradually released. In small groups, you can provide a differentiated experience and personalized support during each step of the process, as shown in table 6.3, ensuring that students are practicing skills with the right level of guidance and support. In a whole-group setting, it is much harder to differentiate instruction and gauge each student's confidence and competence as they move toward independent practice.

### Table 6.3: Differentiating "I Do, We Do, Pairs Do, You Do"

| | *Differentiating "I Do, We Do, Pairs Do, You Do"* |
|---|---|
| **Step 1:**<br>**I do** | **Complexity of content:**<br>• Simplified: For students who need more foundational support, the teacher can break down the content into smaller, more manageable parts, using simpler language and examples.<br>• Advanced: For advanced learners, the teacher can delve into more complex aspects of the content, providing deeper explanations and more sophisticated examples.<br><br>**Visual aids:** Use visuals such as diagrams, charts, images, and videos to complement verbal instructions.<br><br>**Think-alouds:** Vary the complexity of the think-aloud based on student needs, providing simpler explanations for those who need them and more complex ones for advanced learners.<br><br>**Pacing:** Adjust the pace of the demonstration to ensure all students can follow along. Provide pauses for students to ask questions or take notes. |
| **Step 2:**<br>**We do** | **Scaffolded support:** Provide different levels of support within groups. Some groups may need step-by-step guidance, while others might require only occasional check-ins.<br><br>**Interactive tools:** Use interactive tools like whiteboards, apps, or manipulatives to engage students and provide hands-on practice. |
| **Step 3:**<br>**Pairs do** | **Pairing:** Pair students strategically based on their strengths and needs. Pair stronger students with those who need more support, or pair students with similar skill levels to challenge each other.<br><br>**Differentiated tasks:** Provide pairs with tasks that vary in complexity. Some pairs might work on basic tasks, while others tackle more advanced challenges. |

| Step 4: You do | **Choice:** Offer students choices in how they demonstrate their understanding, such as written versus verbal explanations. Give them a choice to select a certain number of problems or tasks to complete.<br><br>**Tiered assignments:** Design assignments with varying levels of difficulty to match student readiness. Provide more straightforward tasks for those who need more practice and complex tasks for advanced learners.<br><br>**Self-pacing:** Allow students to work at their own pace, providing additional time or extensions for those who need it. |
|---|---|

Let's take a look at a second- and third-grade ELA example of "I do, we do, pairs do, you do"!

## *Elementary ELA Example: "I Do, We Do, Pairs Do, You Do"—Making Predictions While Reading*

**Lesson objective:** Students will learn to make predictions while reading by using clues from the text and illustrations to anticipate what might happen next.

### *Step 1: I Do—Teacher Models Making Predictions*

Begin by introducing a short picture book (e.g., *The Snowy Day* by Ezra Jack Keats). Read the first few pages aloud and stop at a key moment to model making a prediction. You might say, "Hmm, I see Peter is putting on his snowsuit and heading outside. I predict that he's going to play in the snow. What clues help me make this prediction?"

Opportunity for differentiation:
- Simplified: Use pictures from the book and model simple, straightforward predictions based on the illustrations and text.
- Advanced: Ask students to consider more complex clues (e.g., Peter's emotions or earlier events) to make their predictions.

## Step 2: We Do—Teacher and Students Make Predictions Together

Continue reading the book, pausing at key moments and asking students to make predictions. You might ask, "What do you think will happen when Peter starts walking through the snow?" or "What do you think Peter will do with the snowball he brought inside?" The class discusses their predictions, with you guiding them to use evidence from the text and pictures.

Opportunity for differentiation:
- Simplified: Provide sentence starters for students needing support (e.g., I predict that __ because __).
- Advanced: Ask students to explain how multiple clues led to their predictions or ask, "What might happen next based on how Peter reacted earlier?"

## Step 3: Pairs Do—Students Make Predictions in Pairs

Divide students into pairs and give them a different short book or passage (e.g., *Frog and Toad Are Friends* by Arnold Lobel). As students read, direct them to pause at specific points to discuss what they think will happen next. Each pair makes predictions and explains their prediction using clues from the text.

Opportunity for differentiation:
- Simplified: Provide simpler texts with more obvious clues and prompts for discussion.
- Advanced: Encourage pairs to predict multiple possible outcomes and compare which one is more likely based on the story's progression.

## Step 4: You Do—Independent Practice

Allow students to continue reading independently. As students read, ask them fill out a prediction chart where they:

- Write down a prediction for what will happen next

- Note the clues from the text or pictures that support their prediction
- Reflect (after reading further) on whether their prediction was accurate and explain why

Opportunity for differentiation:
- Simplified: Give students a prediction worksheet with sentence frames (e.g., I think __ will happen because __).
- Advanced: Encourage students to write down multiple predictions and reflect on which one was the most accurate and why.

## *Teacher-Led Instructional Strategy #2: Hook the Group*

This instructional strategy, called "hook the group," is designed to pique student interest, leverage natural curiosity, engage the group in productive struggle, and encourage learners to communicate, collaborate, and creatively problem-solve with their peers.

Instead of beginning with the instruction or model, you begin by presenting students with an unfamiliar problem, task, or question that gives them time to wrestle with a new challenge and see what they can figure out on their own. The goal is to get students to think critically, problem-solve, think outside the box, tap into strategies they've used in the past, and lean on their peers as resources. A wonderful byproduct of starting a teacher-led station with a hook is that when you get to the instruction or model, students are much more interested in the information presented because they've been engaged in a productive struggle. Over time, they also build stamina and confidence when approaching unfamiliar challenges instead of immediately shutting down. How does hook the group work?

### Step 1: Present the Group with an Unfamiliar Problem, Task, or Question

Begin by introducing a challenge or problem that students have never encountered before. The task should be complex enough to push students to think deeply and apply prior knowledge but not so difficult that they become discouraged.

### Step 2: Pair Students or Divide the Group for a Productive Struggle

Put your students in pairs or break your small group in half and give them time to wrestle with the problem or challenge with peer support. This stage encourages students to engage in a productive struggle where they attempt to work through the unfamiliar task. While they work, listen, and observe, you will note the strategies being used, the questions being asked, and the gaps or misconceptions that surface.

### Step 3: Guide a Quick Debrief

After students have had time to grapple with the hook, lead a short debrief. This could include sharing strategies, surfacing their thinking, discussing roadblocks, and highlighting creative approaches. The goal is for students to reflect on their thinking process and gain insights from their peers.

### Step 4: Follow with the Instruction and Modeling

Once students have engaged with the problem and reflected on their experience, step in to offer targeted instruction and modeling. At this stage, clarify any misconceptions and provide guidance on how to approach similar challenges in the future.

Using this strategy in small, teacher-led instructional sessions allows you to closely observe students' problem-solving processes. This setup enables you to listen more effectively to individual students' strategies, questions, and reasoning, making it easier to identify strengths, gaps, and misconceptions. By contrast, a whole-group instructional session limits the teacher's ability to assess each student's thinking, reducing the opportunity for targeted support and immediate feedback. Table 6.4 highlights how you can differentiate at each step of this strategy.

Table 6.4: Differentiating Hook the Group

| | Differentiating Hook the Group |
|---|---|
| **Step 1: Present the unfamiliar problem/task** | **Complexity of problem/task:**<br>• Simplified: Present a task with fewer variables, clear structure, and direct instructions to help students focus on a single aspect of the concept, skill, or process.<br>• Advanced: Introduce a more complex, open-ended task that allows advanced students to explore multiple approaches, adding layers of complexity as needed. |
| **Step 2: Productive struggle (pairs or small groups)** | **Support during struggle:**<br>• Scaffolded: For students needing more support, provide guiding questions or sentence stems to help structure their thinking. Periodically check in with these groups to provide encouragement and misunderstandings.<br>• Independent: For advanced learners, offer minimal intervention, encouraging them to dive deeper into the challenge and explore alternative solutions. |
| **Step 3: Guide a quick debrief** | **Varied questioning:**<br>• Simplified: Students can share simple solutions or strategies they used, focusing on what worked or what they learned from the task.<br>• Advanced: Ask advanced students to evaluate multiple approaches, compare strategies, and reflect on how they might improve their problem-solving process next time. |

| Step 4: Follow with instruction and modeling | Tailored instruction:<br>• Simplified: Provide explicit instruction with clear models and examples. Use step-by-step demonstrations with simpler language and visual aids.<br>• Advanced: Provide deeper, more complex explanations that push advanced learners to explore more sophisticated applications or real-world connections. |
|---|---|

Let's take a look at a high school math example of the hook the group strategy in action!

## *High School Math Example: Hook the Group—Finding the Area of a Polygon*

**Lesson objective:** Students will explore strategies for finding the area of an irregular polygon, using their prior knowledge of area formulas for other shapes. This session is aligned with the high school math standard HSG.GMD.A.1 (give an informal argument for the formulas for the circumference of a circle, area of a circle, volume of a cylinder, pyramid, and cone).

## *Step 1: Present the Group with an Unfamiliar Problem*

Provide each group with an irregular polygon on graph paper, challenging students to calculate the area. Remind students that they have previously learned how to find the area of basic shapes (e.g., rectangles, triangles, and circles), but they have not been taught how to calculate the area of irregular polygons. Encourage them to think creatively and use each other as resources.

Opportunity for differentiation:
- Simplified: Offer a simpler polygon that can be broken down into more familiar shapes (e.g., a square and triangle).
- Advanced: Provide a more complex polygon that cannot easily be decomposed and might require advanced strategies (e.g., subtraction of areas or integration).

## Step 2: Encourage Productive Struggle in Pairs

Students work in pairs or small groups to solve the problem. Encourage them to break the polygon down into shapes they know how to calculate the area for, or suggest they attempt other strategies based on their previous learning.

Opportunity for differentiation:
- Scaffolded: Offer sentence starters or guiding questions like "How could you divide this shape into smaller, familiar shapes?" or "Can you find any symmetry in the polygon?"
- Independent: Give students minimal guidance, allowing them to explore methods like using coordinates to calculate the area.

## Step 3: Guide a Quick Debrief

After students have spent time grappling with the problem, facilitate a short debrief. Students discuss their approaches and challenges. Invite pairs to share strategies, such as dividing the shape into triangles and rectangles, using the grid on graph paper, or even calculating approximate areas by counting squares.

Opportunity for differentiation:
- Simplified: Focus on clarifying misconceptions or encouraging students to reflect on how they could approach the problem differently next time.
- Advanced: Prompt students to compare strategies and reflect on which approaches were the most efficient or accurate.

## Step 4: Follow with Instruction and Modeling

Provide explicit instruction on calculating the area of irregular polygons, modeling two key strategies:

1. Decomposing the polygon into simpler shapes and summing the areas.

2. Using the coordinate plane and applying the shoelace theorem or integration for more complex shapes.

Opportunity for differentiation:
- Simplified: Model the simpler decomposition method in a step-by-step format with clear, simple visuals.
- Advanced: Demonstrate the application of more sophisticated techniques, such as the coordinate geometry method, and invite students to explore real-world applications (e.g., architecture or land surveying).

## *Teacher-Led Instructional Strategy #3: Concept Attainment*

The concept attainment model is a powerful instructional strategy designed to leverage students' natural curiosity while promoting critical thinking and deeper conceptual understanding. By analyzing examples and non-examples of a concept, students are encouraged to compare, contrast, and identify patterns, helping them to develop a more nuanced understanding of the characteristics that define the concept. This model not only strengthens students' ability to make inferences and recognize patterns, but it also builds their conceptual knowledge. How does the concept attainment model work?

## *Step 1: Present Examples and Non-Examples*

Introduce a series of examples and non-examples related to a particular concept. These can be visual representations, descriptions, or definitions. Each example is labeled as either "Yes" (example) or "No" (non-example), but do not explicitly tell the students the concept they are working toward identifying. The students' job is to determine what characteristics are common among the examples and what sets the non-examples apart.

### Step 2: Encourage Collaborative Discussion

Students work with a partner or within their small group to analyze the examples and non-examples. They ask themselves:

- What do the examples have in common?
- What are the common parts, attributes, or characteristics?
- How are the non-examples different from the examples?

As they discuss, students compare their thinking, contrast the characteristics they observe, and attempt to identify patterns that help define the concept.

### *Step 3: Debrief and Clarify the Concept*

After students have had time to discuss and hypothesize, lead a debrief. Facilitate a discussion where students share their observations and ideas about the concept and ask probing questions to help them refine their thinking. Once students have shared, clarify the concept, highlighting key characteristics and correcting any misconceptions.

Differentiating the concept attainment model in small groups, as described in table 6.5, allows you to better gauge individual students' understanding of the concept and tailor instruction to meet their specific needs. Working in pairs or small groups fosters more equitable discussions, giving every student an opportunity to actively engage with the examples and non-examples, whereas with whole-group instruction, it is difficult to assess each student's thinking.

Table 6.5: Differentiating the Concept Attainment Model

## Differentiating the Concept Attainment Model

| | |
|---|---|
| **Step 1: Present examples and non-examples** | **Complexity of examples:**<br>• Simplified: Use clear, straightforward, concrete examples and non-examples with fewer variables or characteristics for students needing more support.<br>• Advanced: Provide more abstract, complex examples and non-examples with multiple attributes, challenging advanced students to dig deeper into the nuances of the concept. |
| **Step 2: Encourage collaborative discussion** | **Level of guidance:**<br>• Scaffolded: Offer guiding questions, sentence starters, or visual supports (e.g., T-chart) to help students who need more assistance to identify key characteristics and patterns.<br>• Independent: Encourage more advanced students to work with minimal guidance, asking them to uncover multiple patterns or characteristics in the examples. |
| **Step 3: Debrief and clarify the concept** | **Tailored questioning:**<br>• Simplified: During the debrief, ask students needing more support to focus on basic observations such as identifying the most obvious characteristics of the examples. Follow up with direct instruction that reinforces key features using visuals or anchor charts.<br>• Advanced: Challenge advanced students with deeper, more probing questions that require them to explain complex patterns or hypothesize about more sophisticated elements of the concept. Extend instruction by inviting them to explore nuances, exceptions, or how the concept connects to broader ideas or real-world contexts. |

Let's look at an NGSS-aligned elementary science example using the concept attainment model. This example focuses on the second-grade NGSS standard: 2-PS1-1 (plan and conduct an investigation to describe and classify different kinds of materials by their observable properties).

## Elementary Science Example: Concept Attainment Model— Properties of Materials

**Lesson objective:** Students will classify materials based on observable properties (e.g., texture, color, hardness, flexibility) and identify patterns among different materials.

## Step 1: Present Examples and Non-Examples

Present a series of examples and non-examples related to flexibility. For example, objects such as a rubber band, plastic ruler, and cloth are labeled as examples ("Yes"), while a glass cup, wooden block, and metal spoon are labeled as non-examples ("No"). Students are not told the concept is "flexibility" and must analyze the similarities among the examples and the differences of the non-examples.

Opportunity for differentiation:
- Simplified: Provide fewer examples and non-examples, and use clear, easily recognizable objects. Include visual aids or manipulatives for students who may benefit from tactile exploration.
- Advanced: Use more abstract materials that require deeper analysis. Challenge students with more subtle examples and non-examples that may not be as obvious.

## Step 2: Encourage Collaborative Discussion

Pair students to analyze the examples and non-examples, prompting pairs to identify the patterns and characteristics that set the two groups apart. They may discuss questions like:

- What do all the "Yes" objects have in common?
- What do you notice about the "No" objects?
- How are they different?

Opportunity for differentiation:
- Scaffolded: Provide guiding questions, sentence frames, or graphic organizers to help students who need more support structure their discussion (e.g., I think all the "Yes" objects are __ because . . . ).
- Independent: Advanced students may work with minimal guidance and be asked to uncover multiple characteristics of the examples or draw connections to prior learning (e.g., comparing flexibility to another property like hardness).

### *Step 3: Debrief and Clarify the Concept*

Lead a whole-class debrief where students share their ideas and hypotheses. Reveal the concept of flexibility and explain how flexible materials can bend or change shape while rigid materials cannot. Provide additional instruction, giving further examples and non-examples to reinforce the concept. Students may categorize new objects based on their flexibility.

Opportunity for differentiation:
- Simplified: Ask students needing more support to explain basic observations. Provide additional visuals or manipulatives to further illustrate the concept.
- Advanced: Challenge students to think critically about exceptions or nuanced cases. Encourage them to categorize more complex materials or discuss the concept in real-world contexts.

### *Teacher-Led Instructional Strategy #4: Real-Time Formative Feedback*

Formative feedback is information shared with learners to help them refine their thinking or approaches to a specific task, which improves learning outcomes. The real-time formative feedback strategy is designed to provide targeted, immediate support to students as they work, ensuring they receive actionable feedback during the learning process when it is most effective.[4]

While teachers may also use insights from student performance to adjust their instruction, formative feedback primarily targets the learner, offering guidance tailored to their needs. Task-level feedback focuses on providing specific, timely information about a student's response to a given task. Unlike general summary feedback, task-level feedback is immediate and precise, addressing a student's current understanding and skill level.[5] For example, a student struggling with a concept might receive feedback that offers detailed explanations and support, while a proficient student might be challenged to extend their thinking or deepen their understanding.

By dedicating the teacher-led station to focused formative feedback, teachers can identify students who need additional instruction, guide their learning as they work, and prioritize the process of revision. This strategy keeps feedback focused and specific, which motivates students to act on it immediately, reducing the burden of written feedback outside of class and lightening the teacher's workload. How does real-time formative feedback work?

## *Step 1: Focus on a Single Skill or Element of the Student's Work*

To make the most of the time, narrow the feedback focus to one skill or element of the student's work. For example, if the goal is to improve students' use of topic sentences in writing, all feedback will center on that skill, allowing students to receive clear, actionable feedback on a specific aspect of their work, providing guidance on how to improve it.

## Step 2: Provide Students with a Routine for Capturing Questions

As students work on the assignment in progress, they are encouraged to capture their questions using a designated routine or tool (e.g., adding comments in a digital document or writing on a Post-it). This ensures that students do not interrupt the teacher's train of thought during a real-time feedback session.

## Step 3: Keep Your Eye on the Clock

Timing is key in a real-time feedback session. Set clear time limits for reviewing each student's work and offering feedback, ensuring all students receive feedback within the session. This quick, focused feedback is designed to be impactful without overwhelming the teacher or the student.

## Step 4: Use Technology to Speed Up Feedback

To streamline the process, you can leverage technology, creating keyboard shortcuts or making short video tutorials for common or repeated errors. Technology can speed up the feedback process and make it easier to provide consistent, clear guidance to each student.

## Step 5: Require Students to Act on Feedback During the Session

The session does not end with feedback; it ends with action. Students must act on feedback immediately, revising their work or addressing the specific element discussed. This immediate revision cycle reinforces learning and allows students to improve their work in real time while the teacher is still available for additional guidance as needed.

The real-time formative feedback strategy is most effective in small groups because it allows the teacher to provide focused, individualized support and ensures that each student receives timely, actionable feedback, as pictured in table 6.6. In a small-group setting, the teacher can dedicate time to each student's specific needs, offering immediate guidance that students can act on during the session to improve their work. By contrast, a whole-group approach would make it difficult for the teacher to provide targeted feedback to every student, and students might not feel motivated or confident enough to revise their work without that personalized support.

**Table 6.6: Differentiating Real-Time Formative Feedback**

| *Differentiating Real-Time Formative Feedback* | |
|---|---|
| **Step 1: Focus on a single skill or element** | **Complexity of focus:**<br>• Simplified: Focus on a more foundational skill or element for students who need more support.<br>• Advanced: Focus on a more complex skill for advanced students, providing deeper, more nuanced feedback. |
| **Step 2: Provide students with a routine for capturing questions** | **Level of structure:**<br>• Scaffolded: For students who need more support, provide a structured routine, such as sentence starters or a graphic organizer, to help them capture their questions as they work.<br>• Independent: Encourage advanced students to seek answers to their questions by working with a peer, conducting an online search, or analyzing a sample. |
| **Step 3: Keep your eye on the clock** | **Adjusting time for feedback:**<br>• Allow more time for students who need additional explanation or examples to fully grasp the feedback. |
| **Step 4: Use technology to speed up feedback** | **Level of technology support:**<br>• Use technology features like a comment bank of suggestions or questions that target the element or skill of focus for this feedback round.<br>• Record short video tutorials or explanations to support students in making meaningful revisions. |
| **Step 5: Require students to act on feedback during the session** | **Level of revision required:**<br>• Simplified: For students needing more support, guide them in making smaller, more focused revisions.<br>• Advanced: Challenge advanced students to apply the feedback across their entire piece of work or make more sophisticated revisions based on feedback. |

Let's look at a high school writing example, focusing on teaching students how to write informational texts aligned with CCSS. ELA-LITERACY.W.9-10.2. (Write informative/explanatory texts to examine and convey complex ideas, concepts, and information clearly and accurately through the effective selection, organization, and analysis of content.)

## High School English Example: Real-Time Formative Feedback—Writing Informational Texts

**Lesson objective:** Students will draft a clear, well-structured informational text that conveys complex ideas using appropriate structure, transitions, and supporting evidence, receiving real-time feedback to strengthen key elements of their writing.

### Step 1: Focus on a Single Skill or Element

Narrow the feedback focus to one element of informational writing, such as structure (introduction, body, conclusion), organization of ideas, or use of evidence. For example, focus might be placed on the clarity of topic sentences or the coherence between claims and supporting details.

Opportunity for differentiation:
- Simplified: Focus on helping students structure a single paragraph using a graphic organizer with prompts for topic sentence, evidence, and explanation.
- Advanced: Offer feedback on the logical flow between paragraphs or how effectively transitions and domain-specific vocabulary enhance cohesion and clarity.

### Step 2: Provide Students with a Routine for Capturing Questions

Invite students to ask questions by adding comments to their document. For example, they can identify one area they'd like help with (e.g., "Does my evidence clearly support my claim?" or "Is my introduction engaging and focused?"). This encourages self-reflection and helps tailor feedback to their individual needs.

## Step 3: Keep Your Eye on the Clock

Dedicate short time frames (e.g., three minutes) to provide focused, formative feedback on each student's draft. This approach ensures every student receives personalized guidance, maximizes the impact of the teacher-led station, and gives students an immediate opportunity to revise and improve their work.

Opportunity for differentiation:
- Simplified: Spend a bit more time breaking down feedback and modeling revisions with students who need support connecting structure to meaning.
- Advanced: Offer brief, targeted feedback that prompts students to revise independently, or challenge them to evaluate their structure using a checklist or rubric.

## Step 4: Use Technology to Speed up Feedback

Leverage tools like Google Docs comments, Microsoft Word track changes, or AI-assisted writing tools to provide quick, targeted, actionable feedback on structure, transitions, and clarity.

Opportunity for differentiation:
- Simplified: Use prewritten comment banks or drag-and-drop rubrics to provide clear, focused feedback on paragraph structure, clarity, or evidence.
- Advanced: Offer feedback that pushes students to improve word-choice sophistication, tighten arguments, or experiment with different organizational strategies.

## Step 5: Require Students to Act on Feedback During the Session

Students revise their drafts in real time, using the feedback they've received to refine their ideas, organization, or use of evidence.

Opportunity for differentiation:
- Simplified: Ask students to revise just one paragraph or specific section based on feedback, using guided scaffolds like color-coded templates.
- Advanced: Challenge students to revise larger sections of their draft using the feedback they've received, paying special attention to structure, clarity, and word choice.

## Teacher-Led Instructional Strategy #5: Present-Pause-Discuss-Adjust

The present-pause-discuss-adjust strategy is designed to improve student engagement, understanding, and retention of new information by breaking down the presentation of content into manageable chunks. This allows students to absorb information gradually, reflect on their understanding, and ask questions, ensuring that no student is left behind in the learning process. By presenting for about three to five minutes at a time, you can avoid overloading students with too much content all at once. The pause provides an opportunity for students to process what they've heard, fill in their notes, and identify any questions or misunderstandings. This helps both the teacher and the students adjust before moving forward, fostering a more interactive and collaborative learning environment. How does the strategy work?

## Step 1: Present Information in Bite-Sized Chunks

Begin by presenting a small chunk of new information (three to five minutes of explanation at a time). This could be a brief explanation, a visual model, or a demonstration. The key is to keep the presentation short and focused, allowing students to absorb the information without feeling overwhelmed or experiencing cognitive overload.

## Step 2: Pause for Reflection and Note-Taking

After the brief presentation, pause to allow students time to process the information. Encourage students to fill in their notes, capture their thoughts, and write down any questions they have about the content. This pause ensures students have time to capture accurate notes, think critically, and identify gaps in their understanding.

## Step 3: Discuss and Clarify

Students share any questions or thoughts they captured during the pause. Facilitate a brief discussion, addressing misconceptions, providing further clarification, or offering additional examples as needed. This step ensures that all students are on the same page and have a clear understanding before moving on to the next chunk of content.

## Step 4: Adjust and Move Forward

Based on the discussion and any identified gaps in understanding, adjust the explanation if needed, clarify key points, and provide any additional details before moving on to the next chunk of information. This real-time adjustment allows you to respond to the needs of the small group, ensuring that the content is accessible and understood by all students.

The present-pause-discuss-adjust strategy is more effective in a small, teacher-led station because it allows for more interaction and differentiation, as described in table 6.7. In a small group, the teacher can closely monitor each student's understanding and provide immediate, personalized clarification based on the questions or gaps that surface during the pause. This makes it easier to ensure that every student fully grasps the information before moving on. By contrast, whole-group instruction makes it difficult for the teacher to assess individual understanding and adjust in real time, leaving some students at risk of falling behind without the opportunity for timely intervention. Students may also be reluctant to ask questions in a whole-group setting.

**Table 6.7: Differentiating Present-Pause-Discuss-Adjust**

| *Differentiating Present-Pause-Discuss-Adjust* | |
|---|---|
| **Step 1: Present information in bite-sized chunks** | **Complexity of presentation:**<br>• Simplified: Present smaller, more concrete chunks of information with visual supports or demonstrations.<br>• Advanced: Present slightly larger chunks or more abstract material, asking students to connect this information to prior knowledge or consider real-world applications. |
| **Step 2: Pause for reflection and note-taking** | **Level of guidance:**<br>• Scaffolded: Provide note-taking templates, sentence stems, or guiding questions to help students organize their thoughts and capture their understanding during the pause.<br>• Advanced: Allow advanced students to take notes in any format that works for them and encourage them to make connections as they reflect on the information. |
| **Step 3: Discuss and clarify** | **Discussion support:**<br>• Scaffolded: Guide students who need support with specific questions and prompts to encourage participation and clarify their understanding.<br>• Advanced: Challenge advanced students with more complex questions or ask them to lead parts of the discussion, explaining concepts to their peers. |
| **Step 4: Adjust and move forward** | **Level of adjustment:**<br>• Simplified: For students needing more support, reteach or provide additional examples and concrete explanations before moving on.<br>• Advanced: For advanced students, offer more complex examples, extend the discussion, or provide opportunities for them to apply the information in new or challenging contexts. |

Let's take a look at a high school government class focused on determining the central ideas or information of a primary or secondary source.

### High School Government Class Example: Present-Pause-Discuss-Adjust—Understanding the Constitution

**Lesson objective:** Students will learn to analyze key sections of the US Constitution and summarize the central ideas, connecting the historical context to the document's lasting influence on modern government.

### Step 1: Present Information in Bite-Sized Chunks

Present a short section of the Constitution, such as Article I, Section 8, which details the powers of Congress. Explain the text for approximately three to five minutes, breaking down complex legal language and providing historical context for how these powers were originally intended to function.

Opportunity for differentiation:
- Simplified: Present smaller, more digestible portions of the text, providing simpler explanations and a word bank of key terms.
- Advanced: For advanced students, the teacher can delve into more nuanced interpretations of the text, encouraging connections to modern applications or comparisons with other governmental systems.

### Step 2: Pause for Reflection and Note-Taking

After presenting the section, pause for students to reflect on what they've learned. Direct students to take notes, summarize the central ideas, and write down any questions they have about the text or its meaning.

Opportunity for differentiation:
- Scaffolded: Provide students with sentence frames or guided note-taking templates to help them capture key ideas and formulate questions.
- Advanced: Encourage students to take detailed notes independently, asking them to make connections to other historical documents or contemporary issues.

### *Step 3: Discuss and Clarify*

Facilitate a discussion, asking students to share their questions and thoughts on the powers of Congress as described in the Constitution. Clarify any points of confusion, provide additional examples, and encourage deeper thinking about the relevance of these powers in today's government.

Opportunity for differentiation:
- Scaffolded: Ask specific, straightforward questions to guide students' understanding (e.g., "What is the one power granted to Congress that you think is most important?").
- Advanced: Challenge students with more complex depth-of-knowledge questions (e.g., "How has Congress's use of these powers evolved over time?").

### *Step 4: Adjust and Move Forward*

Based on the discussion and any gaps in understanding, adjust the explanation, provide additional clarification or examples as needed, and then move on to the next chunk of the Constitution, such as Article II, which outlines the powers of the executive branch.

Opportunity for differentiation:
- Simplified: Offer a more concrete summary of the section before moving on, ensuring clarity.

- Advanced: Ask students to apply the information by predicting potential conflicts between the powers of Congress and the executive branch based on the text.

The goal of present-pause-discuss-adjust is to transform the transfer of information from a passive to an active experience for students. Instead of sitting silently taking notes for an extended period, they are actively engaged throughout the process and encouraged to ask questions.

## Summary

As educators, our goal is to create learning environments where all students can thrive, and the teacher-led station offers a powerful way to accomplish that goal. By utilizing a variety of small-group instructional strategies, you can address a range of learning objectives and student needs, ensuring that instruction is dynamic, responsive, and engaging. The goal is not simply to transfer information but also to create opportunities for meaningful interactions and deep learning. By tailoring our approach to meet the needs of our students, we can differentiate instruction, build stronger relationships, and make learning more accessible.

The teacher-led station allows educators to elevate Tier 1 instruction, ensuring that first instruction is as effective as possible. With the right strategies, teachers can move beyond one-size-fits-all instruction and instead foster an inclusive, engaging, and collaborative learning environment where all students can progress toward firm, standards-aligned learning objectives.

## Reflect and Discuss

1. What potential barriers do you see in your current approach to whole-group instruction that might make it difficult for

some students to acquire new information? How could small-group instruction address these barriers?

2. How could using a variety of small-group instructional strategies, such as real-time formative feedback or present-pause-discuss-adjust, help you better differentiate for the diverse needs of your students?
3. In what ways can the teacher-led station be used to proactively improve Tier 1 instruction, reducing the need for Tier 2 or Tier 3 interventions?
4. How do you currently assess whether students are engaging meaningfully with the content? How could strategies like hook the group or concept attainment create more opportunities for critical thinking and collaboration?
5. What steps can you take to ensure that the teacher-led station in your classroom is not just a space for transferring information but a place for engaging students, building relationships, collecting formative assessment data, and actively supporting learning?
6. How might incorporating regular, targeted real-time feedback in your small-group instruction improve student motivation and academic growth? What challenges might you encounter, and how can you address them?

## Time to Apply: Design a Small-Group, Teacher-Led Station

**Objective:** In this activity, you will design a small-group, teacher-led station to address a specific learning objective or standard, incorporating pre-assessment, grouping strategies, and differentiation.

## Step 1: Identify the Learning Objective or Standard

Select a learning objective or standard you want to focus on in your small-group, teacher-led station. What do you want your students to learn, understand, or be able to do by the end of the session?

## Step 2: Select a Pre-Assessment Strategy

Choose a pre-assessment strategy to determine what your students already know or can do in relation to the objective or standard. This could be a pre-quiz, an exit ticket, or a discussion prompt. How will you gather this data to inform your instruction?

## Step 3: Choose an Instructional Strategy

Review the small-group instructional strategies from this section (e.g., present-pause-discuss-adjust, hook the group, concept attainment). Select one that best aligns with your objective and your students' needs. Why does this strategy fit your learning objective?

## Step 4: Decide on Grouping

Based on your pre-assessment, decide how you want to group your students. Will you group by skill level (homogeneous) or mixed-skill levels (heterogeneous)? What is your rationale for this grouping method?

## Step 5: Plan Differentiation

Complete your plan by following these steps:

- Use the instructional strategy you selected in step 3 to design your teacher-led station. Describe what you will do and what you'll focus on at each step.
- Identify how you will differentiate the learning experience within the small group. Consider specific scaffolds, supports, or challenges you will provide. For example, how will you adjust for students needing more support versus students

ready for more complex tasks? Which strategies will you use to ensure all students are engaged and supported?

CHAPTER 7

# The Online Station and the Four Cs of Twenty-First-Century Learning

## 7,000 Miles Away but Closer than Ever

As my daughter entered her senior year, her mind was focused entirely on college applications. She knew the process would require an immense amount of time, balancing essays, deadlines, and her demanding academic schedule. I assured her I would be there every step of the way, supporting her. As a former English teacher, I had guided countless high school students through the same process. I was confident we could navigate everything together, from tracking application deadlines to brainstorming for the endless writing prompts.

So, when I received an invitation to work with teachers in Egypt and Ghana in the fall of her senior year, when the pressure would be most intense, Cheyenne was understandably upset. "You're leaving for two weeks! I have so much college stuff to do. You promised you'd help me!"

At that moment, I felt the pang of guilt that working parents know all too well. Balancing my passion for my work with the demands of motherhood has always been a challenge. After taking a deep breath, I assured her that despite the seven thousand miles between us, we would still work together and tackle her applications, just in a different way.

Over the next two weeks, technology became our lifeline. She would share her writing drafts with me via Google Docs, where we could collaboratively brainstorm and refine her ideas. I recorded Loom videos, providing detailed feedback on her essays as if I were sitting right next to her. She'd leave notes on our shared college tracker spreadsheet in the afternoons, and I'd respond in the early mornings before my sessions began in Cairo or Accra. The distance that once seemed like a barrier quickly dissolved as we used these tools not just to communicate but to collaborate in meaningful, creative ways.

What could have been an isolating experience turned into a powerful reminder that technology is not simply a tool for accessing information but a vehicle for human connection. Technology allowed us to strategize, problem-solve, and share ideas from a distance.

Despite its powerful ability to connect us to one another, a lot of the technology used in classrooms isolates learners. They are asked to put on their headphones and watch a video lesson, practice with adaptive software, or complete a digital task alone. I rarely see technology used as a vehicle to cultivate the four Cs of twenty-first-century learning: critical thinking, communication, collaboration, and creativity. I believe that is a missed opportunity. Technology should maximize our students' power and potential, engaging them in tasks that position them to drive their learning.

## Firm Goals

By the end of this chapter, you will:

- Understand the four Cs: critical thinking, communication, collaboration, and creative thinking.
- Learn best practices for designing online learning stations that prioritize the four Cs.
- Grasp how to use technology to provide multiple means of engagement, representation, and action and expression.
- Be able to evaluate the role of technology in a lesson using the SAMR framework.

## Online Learning: Three Key Considerations

Too often, the online station in a Station Rotation Model is underutilized. In some classrooms, it becomes little more than digital busywork—a place to park students while the teacher works with a small group. In others, it's reduced to passive content consumption, like watching videos or completing auto-graded multiple-choice tasks that lack relevance, rigor, or engagement.

To unlock the potential of the online station, we need to shift from using technology as a placeholder to using it as a purposeful design tool. When leveraged well, technology can simplify complex tasks, allow students to learn through a lens of interest, enable content access in various formats, facilitate creation with digital tools, and personalize practice, offering multiple means of engagement, representation, and action and expression. It can also open up opportunities for student voice, choice, and connection.

In a conversation with Paul France for an episode of my podcast, *The Balance*, we discussed technology use, and Paul highlighted three considerations that teachers and instructional coaches should think about when designing online learning[1]:

- Does the technology simplify the task? Does it make it easier (or more complex) for students to complete the task assigned?
- Does the addition of the technology maximize individual power and potential? Does it allow students to do something they could not have done without the technology?
- Does the addition of the technology enhance human connection in a classroom? Does it foster peer-to-peer learning, communication, collaboration, or creativity?

As we design the online learning station in a Station Rotation Model, we need to be proactive in thinking about these questions to ensure that the addition of technology is purposeful and does not present additional barriers that might interfere with the learning activity. We do not want to use technology for technology's sake. We need technology to enhance and elevate the quality of the learning experience.

---

*We do not want to use technology for technology's sake. We need technology to enhance and elevate the quality of the learning experience.*

---

### Targeting the Four Cs of Twenty-First-Century Learning at the Online Station

The four Cs—critical thinking, creativity, collaboration, and communication—are widely recognized as essential skills students need to thrive in the future and succeed in the workplace.[2] These competencies extend beyond academic content and prepare students for real-world challenges, helping them navigate complex problems, adapt to new situations, and engage meaningfully with others. In today's classrooms, where information is readily accessible, the ability to think deeply, express ideas effectively, work in teams, and innovate is more important than ever.

When designing online learning experiences as part of a Station Rotation Model, the four Cs offer a valuable framework for ensuring that technology is used with purpose and intentionality. Rather than simply digitize traditional tasks, we can use the online station to create opportunities for students to solve problems, think creatively, collaborate with peers, and communicate their learning in a variety of formats. These skills not only enhance engagement and deepen understanding, but they also build capacity for lifelong learning.[3] The table below defines each of the four Cs and clarifies what they look like in practice.

**Table 7.1: The Four Cs**

| The Four Cs | What It Means | Online Learning Examples |
|---|---|---|
| **Critical thinking** | This means analyzing and synthesizing information from various sources, evaluating evidence for relevance or bias, and solving problems using logic and reasoning. | Play sorting or matching games on an online platform.<br><br>Analyze an article or online resource and fact-check claims using reliable sources.<br><br>Work with an AI tool to revise and edit work.<br><br>Create a digital concept map or flowchart to understand and organize information.<br><br>Conduct online research to inform decision-making and complete a complex task.<br><br>Engage with a digital simulation that requires decision-making. |

| **Creativity** | This means generating new ideas, exploring different perspectives, and producing original work. | Draw or build a scene or comic with a digital storytelling tool.<br><br>Create a video or podcast to explore or express an idea.<br><br>Design digital storyboards, infographics, or presentations.<br><br>Compose music or digital artwork using online creation tools. |
|---|---|---|
| **Communication** | This means clearly expressing ideas through speaking, writing, or multimedia formats and listening or responding to others. | Engage in asynchronous text-based or video-based discussion.<br><br>Give peer feedback using comments or audio notes.<br><br>Write a blog documenting and reflecting on the learning happening in a class.<br><br>Work on a shared document or slide deck and use a chat feature to discuss progress. |
| **Collaboration** | This means working effectively with others on a shared task or to achieve a shared goal. | Work together to research a topic and create a shared presentation.<br><br>Co-author a piece of writing working on a shared digital document.<br><br>Complete a group project in a shared digital workspace. |

In my coaching sessions, I observe trends in implementation, and it's clear that many emerging technologies can make implementing the four Cs seamless. At the elementary level, for example, students often work with adaptive programs at the online station. These programs encourage critical thinking and are designed to give students more control over the pace of their practice. They also present concepts and skills at a level appropriate to each student's ability level, adjusting individual pathways. These programs not only adapt to the learner's needs, but they also provide teachers with valuable data about student progress, performance, and needs. Despite the benefits of these programs in helping learners develop fundamental skills in areas like reading and math, they are cognitively challenging and often repetitive. If this is the only task younger learners are asked to do in an online station, they may become bored or distracted.

Video lessons are an effective strategy to shift the pace of information acquisition over to learners, allowing them to pause, rewind, and rewatch instruction. Video can also provide your students with opportunities to add closed captioning or adjust the video speed to meet their individual needs better. Unfortunately, videos position students as passive receivers of information unless they are paired with a task that requires students to engage actively with content. Teachers can use programs like Edpuzzle or Nearpod to pair videos with questions or activities designed to get students thinking more deeply. Students can also use reciprocal teaching to engage with a small group to unpack and discuss video content. This inclusive multimedia comprehension strategy encourages students to think critically about and discuss videos. Yet, like adaptive software, if video lessons are the only strategy teachers use to design the online station, students may become bored and disengaged.

The key to designing effective online stations is to use a range of strategies that keep the experience dynamic and interesting for students. Using a variety of tasks at the online station is more likely to keep students interested and motivated to complete those tasks. The online station can help you create more engaging experiences while also teaching critical skills, like online communication, that students will need long after they leave our classrooms.

# The Four Cs in Action at the Online Station

As you consider how to utilize the online station to remove barriers and ensure learning is more accessible, inclusive, and equitable, I challenge you also to use the online station to target at least one of the four Cs. The goal is to avoid designing online learning tasks that position students as passive receivers of information or isolate them in their learning. Instead, students should actively use technology to not only consume and produce but also interact and collaborate, just as I did with my daughter when she needed support during my work trip. Increasingly, colleges and careers leverage technology to connect teams across time and space, fostering collaboration, communication, and creativity, so these skills are invaluable.

Table 7.2 presents strategies you can use to design your online station with the four Cs in mind. Since the four Cs are interconnected, many examples address multiple Cs, allowing you to target more than one skill in a single activity with ease.

**Table 7.2: Understanding the Four Cs**

| The Four Cs | Online Station Ideas |
|---|---|
| **Critical thinking** | **Inquiry-based online exploration:** Provide a high-interest and open-ended question or real-world problem for students to investigate. Ask students to explore multiple resources (curated or researched), gather evidence, synthesize information from multiple sources, and draw conclusions.<br><br>**Thinking routines paired with digital media:** Ask students to view, watch, or listen to various forms of digital media (e.g., infographics, political cartoons, documentary clips, simulations, interactive maps, etc.) and complete a thinking routine like See, Think, Wonder or Connect, Extend, Challenge. |

| | |
|---|---|
| **Communication** | **Online discussions:** Present rich ideas—such as analysis, compare/contrast, cause/effect, synthesis, reflection, or debate questions—in an online discussion forum and allow students the time and space to craft a response, read the responses of their peers, and reply thoughtfully to one another.<br><br>**Reciprocal teaching strategy:** Encourage students to use the reciprocal teaching strategy to engage deeply with online media, such as videos, podcasts, or articles. Each student assumes a specific role—predictor, questioner, summarizer, and clarifier—and uses their role to guide a discussion. As they read, watch, or listen, students should pause at regular intervals (e.g., after each paragraph of text or minute of video) to analyze and discuss content through their comprehension lens. This collaborative process helps students actively process the information, develop deeper comprehension, and improve their speaking and listening skills as they engage with the media. |
| **Collaboration** | **Building background activities:** Ask a group of students to work collaboratively to explore resources (curated or researched) to understand a topic, time period, historical figure, phenomenon, process, or issue. Then, ask them to work together to create a shared online or offline product that shows what they learned (e.g., poster, timeline, slide deck, concept map).<br><br>**Collaborative problem-solving:** Design tasks or challenges that require students to work together to solve a complex problem or complete a challenge. This can involve online research, documentation of work using collaboration tools, and video explanations of findings. |

| Creativity | **Multimedia storytelling:** Ask students to create multimedia projects that combine various forms of communication (e.g., text, images, audio, and video), challenging them to communicate complex ideas in a creative, engaging way. |
| --- | --- |
| | **Digital gallery walk:** Encourage students to showcase their creative projects by posting them online using tools like Padlet, Google Slides, or Seesaw, creating a virtual gallery. The class then explores the gallery and leaves comments, feedback, and questions on each piece. The advantage of a digital gallery walk over a traditional one is that it allows students to showcase diverse multimedia work and receive detailed, asynchronous feedback from peers. It can also be easily shared with families. |

# Dispelling Myths About the Online Learning Station

Despite the growing use of technology in classrooms, persistent myths about the online station continue to shape how it's designed and implemented—often in ways that limit its potential. Many educators have internalized the idea that the technology must be the focus of online work, that every student needs their own device for the station to be effective, or that all students should be doing the same task. These assumptions often result in online stations that prioritize compliance over curiosity, uniformity over personalization, and passive consumption over active engagement. In reality, when technology leads to off-task behaviors, it's usually a reflection of how it's being used, not a flaw in the tool itself.

That's why it's so important to name and challenge these misconceptions about online learning and the role of technology in classrooms. When we shift our thinking and embrace a more nuanced, intentional approach, the online station becomes a powerful tool for differentiation, collaboration, and deeper learning. The myths below—and the realities that follow—illustrate how we can reframe our design choices to maximize the impact of the online learning station in the Station Rotation Model.

## Myth #1: Technology Should Be the Focus of the Online Station

Reality: The online station doesn't need to be device-centric. Instead, it can simply utilize technology as a tool to support and enhance learning. For example, a student may conduct a lab or experiment in a science classroom and use technology to document key parts of the process, capturing photos, time-lapse video, and audio notes to ensure they have comprehensive, accurate multimedia resources to reference when they write a formal lab report. This digital documentation makes it easier for students to draw more accurate and meaningful conclusions from that work.

## Myth #2: Students Must All Have a Device at the Online Station

Reality: It's not necessary for each student to have their own device at the online station. In fact, when students work in pairs or small groups, sharing a device encourages them to engage in meaningful discussions, solve problems together, and negotiate tasks, which reinforces the four Cs. This shared responsibility can lead to more thoughtful use of technology and ensure that students are not passively engaging with the tools but actively interacting with each other and the content.

In addition, limited device access can foster creative solutions. Students may need to divide tasks, alternate roles, or work together more closely, making the learning experience more dynamic and collaborative.

During a class where I was coaching a math teacher implementing the Station Rotation Model, I made an adjustment to the online station that highlighted the benefit of collaboration with shared devices. The original design of the station had each of the six students working on individual devices to review math concepts on the Quizizz platform. As I watched the group, I noticed that none of the students were writing down the math problems and working them out. Instead, they were simply selecting answers and racing through the online practice.

To address that automaticity, I intervened and split the six-student group into two smaller pods of three. Then, I asked two students in each group to put their devices away. This garnered some impressive side-eye! To their credit, they did as I asked. I explained that I wanted them to work together on each question that came up on the screen. First they should work out each problem on their own. Then they should compare their answers. If the group all agreed upon an answer, they could select the one they had all come up with. If they disagreed, they needed to work together to figure out which answer they thought was correct.

This simple adjustment radically changed the energy and experience at that station. Students were working out the problems on paper, discussing their answers, checking each other's work, identifying each other's errors, and chatting up a storm! That station was a powerful reminder that using technology to connect learners with a shared device can actually enhance the quality of their interactions and their learning.

## *Myth #3: All Students Must Work on the Same Task at the Online Station*

Reality: The online learning station is the perfect opportunity to differentiate and personalize the learning experience. You can utilize technology to provide flexible pathways for accessing and acquiring information, online texts, videos, podcasts, or simulations.

You can also use the online station to provide interest-based pathways. For example, a history teacher may invite students to research different aspects of a historical time period or geographic location, allowing students to select the lens of interest (e.g., fashion, government, food, crime and punishment, entertainment). Then, you can invite students to document their learning in a slide deck, digital document, or graphic created with an online design tool.

## UDL Guidelines and the Online Station

UDL emphasizes providing multiple means of engagement, representation, and action and expression to ensure that all students can access, participate in, and demonstrate their learning. While implementing UDL can feel daunting in traditional classroom settings, the online station offers a powerful opportunity to bring these principles to life. When designed intentionally, the online station makes it easier to offer students choice, content variety, and modes to express their learning in alignment with their strengths and needs. The examples in table 7.3 illustrate how each UDL guideline can be activated through thoughtful online station design.

**Table 7.3: Providing Multiple Means at the Online Station**

| UDL Guideline | Online Station Examples |
|---|---|
| **Engagement** | Students research connections to course curriculum through the lens of an interest or through an aspect of their identity, cultural context, or community. |
| | Students access digital texts and online resources that reflect their backgrounds or interests, allowing for deeper personal connections to the material. |
| | Students use digital tools to self-assess work and reflect on student learning and growth. |

| Representation | Students access information via videos, articles, podcasts, infographics, and other forms of digital media to ensure information is accessible.<br><br>Students enlarge text, manipulate audio speed or volume, add closed captioning, etc., ensuring material is accessible for them.<br><br>Students explore digital resources that provide a range of views on a given topic, issue, or event, including different cultural and historical perspectives. |
|---|---|
| Action and expression | Students choose how to express understanding of a concept by writing an essay, creating a video, drawing a comic strip, or designing an infographic.<br><br>Students engage in an asynchronous text- or video-based discussion, depending on the learner's ability and preference.<br><br>Students produce artifacts of learning using a range of digital creation tools to demonstrate learning (e.g., infographics, podcasts, videos, digital slide decks). |

## SAMR Framework

One of the challenges educators face when designing the online station is determining whether technology is being used meaningfully or simply replacing traditional tasks with digital versions that don't add much value. Without clear guidance, it's easy to fall into patterns of low-level tech use that may look innovative on the surface but doesn't actually enhance student learning or engagement. That's where the substitution, augmentation, modification, and redefinition (SAMR) framework, developed by Dr. Ruben Puentedura, is extremely helpful. It provides a useful lens for evaluating how technology is being used and for pushing ourselves to design experiences that move beyond substitution and instead strive for true transformation.[4]

# The Online Station and the Four Cs of Twenty-First-Century Learning

The SAMR framework helps educators think critically about how to use technology to elevate and expand what's possible in the classroom. It encourages a progression from using tech as a direct substitute for paper-based tasks to using it to augment, modify, or even redefine the learning experience entirely. When applied to the online station, SAMR can serve as both a reflection and design tool—helping teachers assess where their current practices fall and consider ways to deepen and enrich learning through more intentional use of digital tools. Table 7.4 illustrates how technology used at the online station can align with each tier of the SAMR framework.

**Table 7.4: The SAMR Framework**

| SAMR Framework | What Is It? | What Does It Look Like? |
| --- | --- | --- |
| **Substitution** | The technology acts as a direct substitute for a traditional offline tool, and there is no real change in the task itself. | Instead of writing an essay by hand, students type the essay on a computer. |
| **Augmentation** | The technology replaces the traditional offline tool and provides functional improvements to the task. | Students type their essays using Google Docs, using tools like voice typing, a dictionary, translation tools, and accessibility features. |
| **Modification** | The technology allows for a significant redesign of the task. | Students collaborate on a shared writing assignment using Google Docs, adding images, providing each other with peer edits in real time, and adding comments and suggestions. Students use AI tools to receive feedback on their writing and make revisions. |
| **Redefinition** | The technology allows for entirely new tasks that were not possible before the addition of the technology. | Students create multimedia digital stories incorporating text, images, audio, and video, and they publish them online for an authentic audience for feedback. |

When designing online stations, you should thoughtfully consider the role technology plays in students' learning experience. By doing so, you will bring a higher level of intentionality to the design process, ensuring that technology enhances, rather than merely replaces, traditional tasks. While the goal is to move beyond simply substituting technology, it's important to remember that progress through the SAMR framework isn't always linear. As you become more proficient with technology, more tasks may fall into the modification and redefinition categories. However, there will still be moments when technology is used best to substitute or augment a task. The key is to stay mindful of how you integrate technology so that you can continually grow in designing online learning activities that maximize impact.

## Summary

In line with UDL Guidelines, the online station should provide students with multiple means of engagement, representation, and expression, ensuring learning is accessible. This approach to the online station creates diverse pathways that cater to different student identities, interests, learning preferences, and needs.

Additionally, you can use the online station to prioritize the four Cs of twenty-first-century learning. By doing so, you can avoid the common pitfall of using technology for isolated, low-interest tasks that fail to engage students.

The SAMR framework offers a valuable lens for evaluating and reflecting on the role of technology in a lesson. Considering the SAMR framework encourages you to continuously refine your technology integration in order to maximize the impact of devices and online tools on student learning.

## Reflect and Discuss

1. How can you ensure that your online stations provide multiple means of engagement, representation, and action and expression to meet the diverse needs of your students? What changes might you make to your current approach to online learning activities?
2. Review table 7.3 and brainstorm additional strategies you can add to your multiple means. How else might you give students meaningful choices at the online station?
3. In what ways can you intentionally design your online stations to foster the four Cs of twenty-first-century learning? Which of these skills do you feel most confident in fostering right now with technology? Which skill or skills would you like to prioritize moving forward?
4. What are some common pitfalls you've encountered when using technology in online stations? How did the information presented in this chapter get you thinking about how you might avoid those in the future?
5. Reflect on a recent online learning task you designed. Where would it fall in the SAMR framework (substitution, augmentation, modification, redefinition)? If it falls under substitution or augmentation, what steps could you take to move it toward modification or redefinition?

## Time to Apply: Design an Online Learning Station

**Objective:** In this activity, you will design an online learning station to address a specific learning objective or standard while targeting one or more of the four Cs (critical thinking, communication, collaboration, or creativity). You'll consider differentiation strategies and the ways technology can enhance students' learning experiences.

## Step 1: Identify the Learning Objective or Standard

Select a learning objective or standard to guide the design of your online station. What do you want students to learn, understand, or be able to do by the end of the station? Ensure that the task you design aligns with this goal and integrates one of the four Cs to deepen learning.

## Step 2: Choose a Four-C Focus

Decide which of the four Cs will be the focus of this online station. How will you leverage technology to develop that skill? To review, the four Cs are:

- **Critical thinking:** Engaging students in problem-solving or analysis tasks
- **Communication:** Facilitating meaningful interactions, such as peer feedback or discussions
- **Collaboration:** Creating opportunities for group work or shared projects
- **Creativity:** Encouraging the creation of original work, like videos, infographics, or digital stories

## Step 3: Select Technology Tools

Identify the digital tools, resources, or platforms that target your chosen C. For example, you might use discussion boards, collaborative documents or slides, or creative design tools. How will the selected tools enhance the learning experience and align with the C you're focusing on?

## Step 4: Plan for Differentiation

Consider how you might differentiate the learning experience at the online station:

- Will students have choices in tasks or resources?

- Will they work at different levels of complexity? For example, you might offer a variety of media types (text, video, audio) or tiered tasks based on students' readiness levels.
- What scaffolds will you provide to support all learners?

### Step 5: Self-Assess Using the SAMR Framework

Once you have designed your online station, use the SAMR framework to reflect on the role of technology within the station. Consider how the technology elevates the learning experience:

- **Substitution:** Is technology simply replacing a traditional tool without changing the task significantly?
- **Augmentation:** Does the technology enhance the task by adding functionality or improving efficiency?
- **Modification:** Does the technology significantly redesign the task, allowing for new ways of learning or completing the activity?
- **Redefinition:** Does the technology enable tasks or learning experiences that would be impossible without it?

Based on this self-assessment, determine if your technology use truly transforms the learning experience. If needed, consider adjustments to push it further along the SAMR framework.

# CHAPTER 8

# The Offline Station and Student Agency

## My Way or the Highway Didn't Instill a Love of Reading

In my first few years as a high school English teacher, I stubbornly insisted that every student annotate each page of the novels we read. Annotating had worked for me as a student, and I assumed it would work for my students, too. And guess what? My students hated it. Every semester, I braced myself for the flood of feedback forms where they complained that the novels were long, boring—and the annotations? The worst. At first, I brushed it off, convinced they needed to buckle down and embrace the struggle.

But after years of watching students groan, procrastinate, and completely disengage from the texts I hoped would spark a love of reading, I finally admitted to myself that something wasn't working. My turning point came when one particularly honest student wrote in their feedback, "I don't hate reading—I hate what you make us read and how you make us do it." Ouch. That one stung, but it also made me think: Maybe the problem wasn't them—maybe it was me.

So, I decided to experiment. I gave up some control (which felt a little terrifying at first), and instead of assigning the same story to everyone, I allowed my students to choose the short stories they read from a list. I also introduced literature circles for one unit each semester. Students got to pick their group's book, set their reading schedule, and engage with the text through discussions and collaborative assignments they designed with their peers.

On top of that, I swapped my rigid annotation mandate for something radical—student choice. I onboarded them to three strategies for active reading: traditional annotations (for the type As like me), sketchnotes (for the artistic and visual students), and dialogic journals (for the writers). Once they had experience and practice with all three, they got to pick the strategy that worked best for them each time they read.

The result? A total one-eighty. Instead of complaining about long, boring books, students completed the reading, discussed characters and themes, and actually enjoyed the experience. My once-dreaded feedback forms were suddenly filled with comments like "I loved this story!" and "Can we do more literature circles next semester?" I even got a few requests for book recommendations.

What I realized was simple but powerful: Reading is personal. Not everyone loves the same stories or types of texts, and not everyone engages with texts in the same way. My job wasn't to force a one-size-fits-all approach; it was to foster a love of reading by giving my students the agency to choose what worked for them. When I did that, they felt more competent, confident, and connected—not just with the texts but with each other.

The impact of giving students agency in the classroom is powerful. Instead of making all the decisions about what's best for your students, empower your students to decide what works best for them.

As they get more comfortable and confident in making decisions, they also learn a lot about themselves.

In this chapter, we'll explore the value of prioritizing student agency and meaningful choice. Obviously, teachers can incorporate agency into any station, but we'll focus on the value of these meaningful choices in the offline learning station. In addition to emphasizing student agency, I will make a case for using the offline station to engage students in meaning-making activities designed to help them process new information. I will also highlight the benefits of using this station to help students stretch their metacognitive muscles and think about their learning in intentional ways.

## Firm Goals

By the end of this chapter, you will:

- Understand the value of providing students with agency and meaningful choices.
- Know how to design offline tasks that provide multiple means of engagement and action and expression.
- Comprehend the role of meaning-making activities and how to embed them into the offline station.
- Be able to boost students' metacognitive awareness with activities and routines designed to get them thinking about their thinking and reflecting on their learning.

## Supporting Student Agency

Learner agency is a key focus in the updated version of the CAST UDL Guidelines. CAST emphasizes the importance of recognizing and building upon the agency students bring with them into the classroom—their ability to make decisions, take ownership of their learning, and act with purpose. Developing learner agency means supporting students in becoming more self-aware, goal directed, and strategic in their approach to learning. When students are given meaningful choices about their learning experiences—what they learn, how they learn it, or how they show what they know—it can significantly increase their motivation, engagement, and sense of ownership.

It's important to understand how empowering student agency also builds student motivation. Self-determination theory, developed by Richard M. Ryan and Edward L. Deci,[1] emphasizes the importance of understanding motivation on a psychological level. It highlights a spectrum of motivation, ranging from externally controlled behaviors to those driven by personal choice and autonomy. Central to this theory are three basic psychological needs: autonomy, competence, and relatedness, as pictured in figure 8.1.

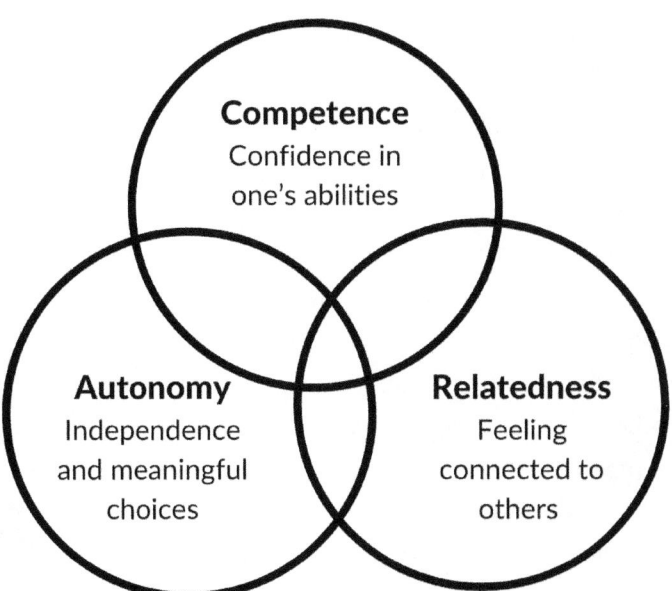

Figure 8.1: Three Psychological Needs Required for Motivation

Let's unpack these three psychological needs in order to understand what they are and why they're important.

**Autonomy** is the human desire to feel in control of one's actions and decisions. It involves a sense of agency and the freedom to make choices that align with one's values, preferences, interests, and goals. Individuals tend to be more motivated, engaged, and fulfilled when they feel they have control over their behaviors and environment rather than feeling compelled to comply with external pressures.

When autonomy is satisfied, people experience greater well-being, creativity, and motivation. By contrast, when autonomy is thwarted, feelings of helplessness, disengagement, and frustration often result. Building agency into a lesson or learning experience can help satisfy students' needs for autonomy and allow them to pursue a task through a lens of interest or from a place of strength.

**Competence** is the level of confidence a person has in their ability to effectively complete specific tasks or navigate an environment. When people feel competent, they are more likely to take on challenges and persist when working through complex tasks. By contrast, a lack of competence can result in a person feeling inadequate, frustrated, and disengaged.

If you only provide one pathway through a learning experience, students may not feel confident in their ability to succeed, and they might shut down. By giving students agency and meaningful choices, we can ensure that they have multiple pathways to choose from, boosting their feelings of competence.

**Relatedness** is the human need to form meaningful connections with others. It encompasses a sense of belonging, being cared for, and caring for others. In the context of education, relatedness entails feeling connected to, and accepted by, an inclusive learning community. When students experience relatedness, they feel understood, valued, and supported by the other members of the learning community. When students are given the autonomy to make decisions about their learning, they feel trusted and valued, strengthening their relationships within the community.

Relatedness fosters feelings of safety and connection, which are critical for emotional well-being and motivation. When people feel connected to those around them, they tend to be more engaged and cooperative. However, when the human need for relatedness is not met, people may feel isolated, lonely, or even alienated.

Teachers can effectively support these three psychological needs by incorporating meaningful choices into their lessons and learning experiences, allowing students to feel in control of their learning journey, competent in their abilities, and connected to you and their peers.

By its nature, the Station Rotation Model requires a higher degree of self-regulation and self-directed learning. Given these increased demands, the value of prioritizing student agency cannot be overstated. When we build in meaningful choices at stations, we help students feel more confident they can complete the task assigned.

At the offline station, providing meaningful choices satisfies students' need for autonomy as students engage in self-directed tasks. Offering multiple pathways boosts students' confidence in completing assigned tasks, enhancing their sense of competence. In collaborative stations, students' need for relatedness is fulfilled as they engage in discussions, collaborate on shared tasks, and solve problems with peers. When students are given agency across various stations, they also develop stronger executive functioning skills—such as managing their time and making decisions—and are more likely to feel motivated and take ownership of their learning.[2]

# A Sustainable Approach to Student Agency

While student agency is a vital component of the Station Rotation Model, you may feel daunted by the time required to generate meaningful choices—especially construct-specific choices aligned with the knowledge, skills, or abilities that a specific task is targeting.

However, teachers shouldn't feel pressure to generate a bunch of different options for students. Research has identified that the sweet spot is two to four options, so it isn't necessary (and can even be counterproductive) to whip up a large number of options.[3] I encourage you to start with a simple "would you rather" option in each lesson or at one station in a rotation.

It can feel difficult to know where to start when embracing student agency. When designing a Station Rotation Model lesson, you may want to consider giving students options related to course content, their process, or the products they create to demonstrate their learning, as depicted in table 8.1.

- **Content choices** allow students to engage with the same material in different ways, such as reading an article versus analyzing an infographic. Content choices can also allow students to choose a lens of interest to pursue their learning. For example, in a history lesson on the Industrial Revolution, students could explore the topic through the lens of technological advancements, focusing on key inventions like the steam engine, or they might choose a social lens, analyzing how factory working conditions impacted labor movements. Content flexibility enables students to engage more deeply with the material in a way that aligns with their interests.
- **Process choices** provide flexibility in how students approach their learning, such as writing a journal entry or participating in a discussion. Process choices can also allow students to make decisions about the steps they move through to complete a task, the materials they use, or whether they work online or offline.
- **Product choices** remove barriers that make it challenging for students to express and communicate their learning accurately. Product choices, from written explanations to

more creative artifacts like recording an original podcast episode, allow students to decide how to successfully share their learning.

Table 8.1: "Would You Rather" Options

| "Would You Rather" Options | | |
|---|---|---|
| | **Option 1** | **Option 2** |
| **Content** | Read a printed article, passage, or textbook excerpt about the topic. Highlight key ideas, take notes, and create a brief written summary or outline to explain what you've learned. | Use printed materials, diagrams, or illustrations to create a concept map, poster, or visual summary of the key ideas. Include captions or labels to explain your thinking. |
| **Process** | Write a paragraph connecting the main ideas in a text, video, or unit of study. | Create a concept map connecting the main ideas in a text, video, or unit of study. |
| **Product** | Write a traditional research paper exploring a topic. | Develop an infographic summarizing the key findings of the research. |

Our students may not have much experience making decisions about their learning, so we want to help them build stamina and confidence in making choices that shape their learning experience. The benefit of using this "would you rather" strategy is that it makes offering students meaningful choices feel manageable for teachers, and it avoids overwhelming students. This emphasis on student agency stands in stark contrast to the design of most traditional lessons, where the entire class, regardless of their diverse needs and interests, is often asked to complete the same tasks with little room for voice or choice.

# Beyond the Worksheet

When I go into classrooms, I usually see pencils and worksheets at the offline station. Review and practice are an important part of reinforcing concepts and skills, but worksheets are unlikely to excite students, especially if they're working independently at an offline station. If worksheets are the only strategy teachers use at the offline station, students may not stay engaged in the task, which may result in unproductive, off-task behaviors.

One of my favorite books, *Powerful Teaching: Unleash the Science of Learning* by Patrice Bain and Pooja Agarwal, emphasizes the crucial role that retrieval practice, spacing, and interleaving play in deepening student understanding. As they explain, "Retrieval practice is the same thing as the retrieval stage of the learning process: It's when we practice bringing information to mind. We tend to think that most learning occurs during the encoding stage, but a wealth of research demonstrates that learning is strengthened during retrieval." Learning isn't solidified when students receive information—it's strengthened when they're asked to use it, which is why our instructional models must create regular, low-stakes opportunities for retrieval across stations and learning experiences.

Retrieval practice can take the form of worksheets. But there are myriad ways to encourage our students to retrieve information from their brains—ways that foster higher-order thinking and increased engagement. Peer-to-peer teaching, problem-solving challenges, or applying learned concepts to real-world scenarios are all ways to actively engage students with the material and make the learning experience more dynamic and interactive.

The beauty of the offline station is the opportunity to engage students in a wide range of tactile, social, and experiential learning designed to help them make meaning and apply knowledge. By offering multiple ways to engage with concepts and skills at the offline station, teachers can effectively implement UDL. Flexible pathways that encourage our students' identities and interests will optimize relevance, value, and authenticity in the learning environment.

## UDL Guidelines and the Offline Station

The offline station is a powerful space for implementing the principles of UDL because it creates space for tactile, interpersonal, and experiential learning that may not always be possible in online or teacher-led settings. It allows students to engage in hands-on tasks, collaborate face-to-face with peers, and interact with physical materials, as pictured in table 8.2. All of this supports multiple means of engagement, representation, and expression.

Whether students are building, sketching, sorting, discussing, or moving, the offline station can be intentionally designed to offer varied pathways for accessing content and demonstrating understanding. These experiences honor learner variability by tapping into different strengths, preferences, and sensory modalities, helping all students feel seen, supported, and capable.

**Table 8.2: Providing Multiple Means at the Offline Station**

| UDL Guideline | Offline Station Examples |
|---|---|
| **Engagement** | • Engage students with texts, topics, or hands-on tasks that connect with their identities and cultural backgrounds.<br>• Include activities that allow students to work independently or in groups on a collaborative challenge, depending on their preference.<br>• Dedicate time to goal-setting and self-reflection using tools like ongoing self-assessment documents and journals to track progress and identify strengths, areas in need of development, and moments of growth. |

| Representation | - Present information through multiple physical forms such as diagrams, models, or tactile tools (e.g., 3-D models, manipulatives).<br>- Include activities that reflect students' diverse cultural backgrounds or personal experiences, like analyzing real-world examples related to the curriculum.<br>- Rotate through stations offering opportunities to interpret information from multiple perspectives, and encourage students to discuss concepts using physical cards or manipulatives to support meaning-making. |
|---|---|
| Action and expression | - Let students express their learning through physical products like drawings, crafts, or models.<br>- Incorporate role-play or debates, encouraging students to physically move, collaborate, and demonstrate understanding.<br>- Create a station with building blocks or materials where students solve a physical challenge related to the lesson.<br>- Let students record their reflections in a written or creative form, such as a visual mind map or design board. |

In addition to offering varied opportunities for engagement, representation, and action and expression, I'll focus on two key strategies for going beyond simple review and practice. First, you can use this station to help students make sense of the content they're learning, encouraging deeper understanding. Second, the offline station can allow students to engage in metacognitive activities that strengthen their executive functioning skills, promoting self-awareness and self-regulation.

## Making Time for Meaning-Making

One of the best ways to reframe the offline station is as a space where students have dedicated time to perform the cognitive work of meaning-making. Meaning-making is the process of interpreting, understanding, organizing, and integrating new information into a person's existing knowledge framework. Students will prefer to process and make meaning in different ways, which is why prioritizing student agency and meaningful choice is so critical to ensuring all students can be successful.

Several cognitive processes are at play when students take in new information and attempt to process it. Initially, information is encoded in the brain, transforming sensory input—what students see, hear, or read—into a form that the brain can store and process. This encoding involves attention and perception, allowing the brain to filter and focus on relevant information. Once information is encoded, the brain links this new information with existing knowledge and experiences stored in long-term memory.[4] This association helps students make connections, facilitating deeper understanding and improving retention.

Elaboration is the process by which students connect new information with what they already know. Elaboration strengthens neural connections, making the new information more meaningful and memorable.[5] It requires that students access their prior knowledge and think deeply about the new concepts, processes, and skills. During elaboration, students actively engage with the new information by analyzing, questioning, and synthesizing it. This could involve discussing the content with classmates, connecting it to real-life examples, or applying it to solve problems. Finally, the brain organizes the information by categorizing and structuring it in a way that makes sense.

Despite the importance of the meaning-making step in the learning process, many lessons jump straight from information transfer (e.g., lecture and mini-lessons) to practice and application (e.g., practice problems and review), without providing students the space to engage in meaning-making. Without dedicated class time and necessary scaffolding, students may struggle to connect new information to their existing knowledge base, making it harder to retain and use. Table 8.3 presents a collection of strategies you can use to help students interpret, organize, and make sense of what they are learning.

**Table 8.3: Meaning-Making Activities: "Would You Rather" Options**

| Meaning-Making Activities: "Would You Rather" Options ||
|---|---|
| **Option 1** | **Option 2** |
| Take traditional notes. | Draw sketchnotes. |
| Join a small-group, in-person discussion. | Journal or write a reflection. |
| Make a list of important concepts. | Use a graphic organizer to organize ideas. |
| Write a paragraph making connections between concepts. | Create a concept map identifying and connecting concepts. |
| Participate in role-playing scenarios. | Create a comic strip or storyboard. |
| Build a physical model or create an image (drawing, collage, painting) to represent a concept or event. | Create an artistic timeline of important events or a flowchart showing a progression. |
| Compare and contrast using a Venn diagram. | Compare and contrast in a paragraph. |
| Complete a 3-2-1 reflection, identifying three things learned, asking two questions, and sharing one thing that was surprising. | Complete the Connect, Extend, Challenge thinking routine, connecting new learning to prior knowledge, explaining how the new information extended thinking, and identifying what was challenging about the new information. |

Some students may prefer individual meaning-making tasks, such as writing a reflection or completing a graphic organizer. Others may thrive by collaborating with their peers, engaging in discussions, or role-playing activities to process the material. Since no single strategy works for all students, offering a "would you rather" format gives your class meaningful choices. This approach empowers students to select the method they feel best supports their understanding, enabling them to make sense of the content and build critical connections between their prior knowledge and new information.

Some teachers express concern that students might make a poor choice or select an "easier" option. However, the goal of offering students agency and meaningful choice is to empower *them* to make decisions about what works best for their learning. This process not only engages students in meaning-making but also helps them develop a deeper understanding of themselves as learners. The most effective way to support students in learning from their choices is to provide opportunities for reflection. By pausing to evaluate the choices they've made—whether the strategy they selected truly helped them understand the content or apply the skill—students will begin to strengthen their metacognitive muscles.

---

*The goal of offering students agency and meaningful choice is to empower them to make decisions about what works best for their learning. This process not only engages students in meaning-making but also helps them develop a deeper understanding of themselves as learners.*

---

This self-reflection is essential in helping students recognize what works, what doesn't, and how to adjust their strategies moving forward.

## Metacognitive Skill-Building Tasks and Executive Functioning

The offline station can also be a space for students to build metacognitive skills. These are essential to the development of executive functioning, which includes the ability to organize tasks, manage time, and sustain focus.[6, 7] By encouraging students to think about their learning and regulate their behavior, you help them develop metacognitive awareness and executive functioning skills.

You can use the offline station to offer students dedicated time to set academic or behavior goals, self-assess their progress, and engage in reflection—practices that can also serve as meaningful communication tools with families. Given the increased focus on executive functioning in CAST's updated guidelines, it's important to understand how closely these skills are tied to student agency. When students are taught to set goals, monitor their progress, and reflect on their learning, they begin to see themselves as active participants in their education—capable of making decisions, adapting strategies, and taking ownership of their growth.

Research shows that students who regularly reflect on their progress and adjust their learning strategies are better equipped to manage their time and attention, which are critical for academic success.[8,9] Designing the offline station with a focus on helping students develop their ability to think about their learning not only promotes self-directed learning, but it also builds the foundational skills students need to thrive when tackling complex tasks.

You can integrate metacognitive routines strategically throughout the learning process—before, during, and after.

## *Before Learning: Goal-Setting and Pre-Planning*
### Goal-Setting

When students set goals, they create a road map for their success, outlining the steps they need to take to achieve their personal, academic, or behavioral goals. This encourages the core skills of self-monitoring and planning.

Ask students to set academic, behavioral, or personal goals. You might have them create a single small goal at the start of each week and then end the week by asking them to revisit their goal and evaluate how much progress they made toward it. Alternatively, you may prefer to have students set a few goals at the start of each unit or grading period and track their progress. The power of goal-setting is that it not only requires the learner to decide what they care about and want to work toward—which is inherently motivating—but it also exercises planning and self-regulation skills, which are key to executive functioning (discussed in more detail later).

Figure 8.2 shows a graphic organizer that you can use to support the goal-setting process. Students use the left-hand column to articulate their goal(s) for the week, unit, or grading period. The center column asks them to think about how they will make progress toward their goal(s), tasking them with describing the actions and behaviors they can commit to. This engages students' self-regulation by helping them identify strategies to stay on track. The right-hand column asks students to reflect on what success will look and feel like—encouraging them to visualize their success, enhancing their motivation to persevere through challenges and setbacks.

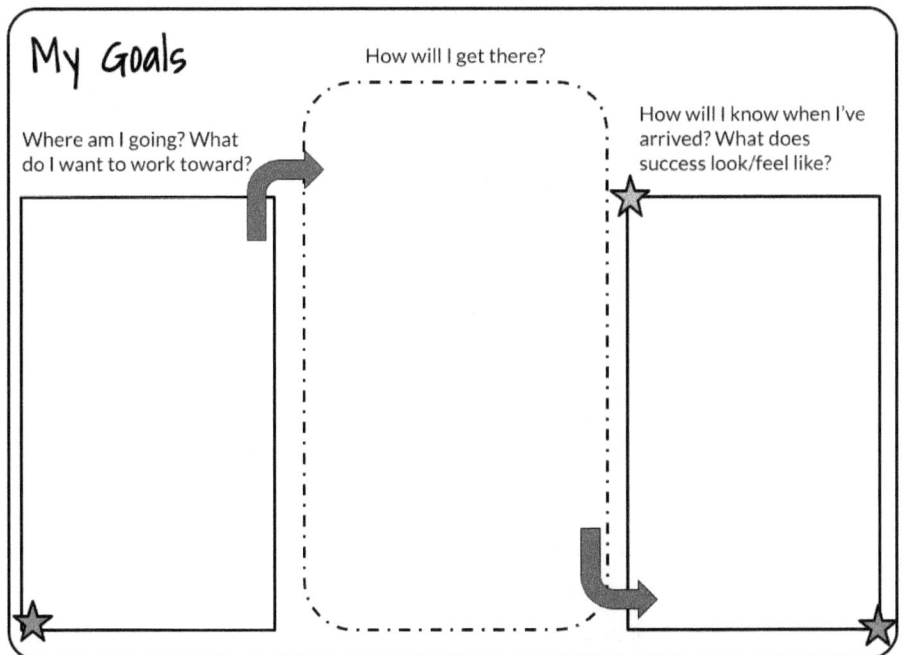

**Figure 8.2: Goal-Setting Graphic Organizer**

## Pre-Planning

When students are about to embark on a new learning experience, large-scale assignment, or project, the offline station can be dedicated to pre-planning and asking students to assess their prior knowledge and available resources, outline a plan or series of steps, and identify areas of confusion or concern where they may need additional support or guidance from you.

For example, imagine a science teacher is assigning a project on ecosystems and biodiversity that students will work on for several weeks. They may ask students to use the offline station to create an initial research plan. This could involve identifying what they already know about ecosystems, listing research questions they want to explore, outlining the resources they plan to use, and mapping out the steps they'll take to complete their project. Additionally, students could reflect on areas where they feel uncertain, such as their ability to conduct credible online research, and note what support or clarification they might need from the teacher to move forward confidently.

Figure 8.3 shows an example of a pre-planning document that teachers can use to engage students in this process.

When students assess their prior knowledge, outline a plan, and identify areas of concern before beginning a project, they exercise the following executive functioning skills:

- **Organization:** Pre-planning requires students to break a large task or project into manageable steps, promoting structured thinking and organizational skills. Students learn to create a road map that guides their actions throughout the assignment.
- **Goal-setting and task initiation:** By outlining the steps to complete a project, students learn how to set goals and initiate tasks effectively—two essential aspects of executive functioning.

**Pre-Planning Document**

| Questions | Answers |
|---|---|
| What is your goal for this assignment? What do you want to accomplish? | |
| What do you already know about this topic, subject, or issue that might be useful as you complete this assignment? | |
| Describe what you plan to do and how you plan to do it. What do you need to do first, second, third, etc.? | |
| What strategies will you use to complete this assignment? | |
| What aspect of this assignment may be challenging for you? If you get stuck, where can you go to get help? | |

Figure 8.3: Pre-Planning Document

- **Self-monitoring:** As students reflect on what they already know and where they feel uncertain, they engage in self-monitoring—a metacognitive process that involves recognizing gaps in knowledge and predicting potential challenges. This reflective practice allows them to be proactive in seeking support and managing obstacles.
- **Cognitive flexibility:** Pre-planning encourages students to anticipate challenges and identify strategies they can use to navigate them, enhancing their ability to adapt when unexpected difficulties arise.

Metacognitive skill-building helps students become more competent, self-directed, and independent learners, better equipped to tackle complex projects and assignments.

## During the Learning: Thinking Routines and Ongoing Self-Assessment

Project Zero[10] has developed an incredibly useful and versatile collection of research-based thinking routines designed to support students. To ensure these thinking routines are accessible to all learners, teachers can provide a collection of sentence stems to help students with language support as they articulate their responses. Teachers may also want to provide the option for students to either write, record, or draw their responses to these questions.

### #1: See, Think, Wonder

Pictured in figure 8.4, the See, Think, Wonder routine asks students to observe closely, interpret their observations thoughtfully, and surface their thinking or generate questions to drive inquiry.

| What do you **see**? | What do you **think**? | What do you **wonder**? |
|---|---|---|
|  |  |  |

**Figure 8.4: See, Think, Wonder Thinking Routine**

This routine starts with the fundamental act of seeing. Encourage students to closely observe images, texts, simulations, artwork, data sets, or any visual material presented to them. This initial step prompts them to engage their senses, paying attention to details they might otherwise overlook. Whether exploring scientific phenomena, literary works, historical events, or visual art, observation is the foundation of deeper exploration and understanding. You can provide students with these prompts:

- I see [specific details or objects].
- I notice [observable patterns or changes].
- I observe [distinctive colors, shapes, or forms].
- I recognize [familiar symbols or icons].

Next comes the thinking stage. Prompt learners to construct meaning, make connections or predictions, and explore possibilities as they reflect on their observations. This critical thinking process encourages them to draw inferences, identify patterns, and make informed interpretations. Whether analyzing literary themes, scientific data, historical evidence, or artistic techniques, this analytical thinking nurtures their ability to approach subjects with a more discerning and insightful lens. Here are some prompts:

- I think this means . . .
- I interpret this as . . .
- I can infer that . . .
- It appears that . . .

The final stage of this thinking routine is wondering. Students generate questions from their observations and interpretations. Encouraging students to ask thought-provoking questions not only fosters a deeper understanding of subject matter, but it also leverages their natural curiosity, inspiring them to seek answers and become lifelong learners. Here are some prompts:

- I wonder why . . .
- What would happen if . . .
- How does this relate to . . .
- I'm curious about . . .

#2: Connect, Extend, Challenge

Shown in figure 8.5, Connect, Extend, Challenge offers students a structured approach for deepening their understanding and reflections. It challenges learners to connect new information to prior knowledge, consider how their learning impacts their thinking, and identify areas of challenge or uncertainty. This routine fosters critical thinking and enhances the meaningful integration of new learning into a student's existing knowledge framework.

| Connect | Extend | Challenge |
|---|---|---|
| How does this **connect** to what you already know? | What new ideas have **extended** your thinking on this topic? | What is **challenging** or confusing? What do you wonder? |
|  |  |  |

Figure 8.5: Connect, Extend, Challenge Thinking Routine

In the connect phase, students anchor new information or ideas to their prior knowledge, making unfamiliar content more accessible. Here are some prompts:

- This reminds me of...
- This is just like the time...
- This connects to my previous knowledge because...
- This is similar to...

Next comes the extend stage. Learners consider how new concepts have pushed the boundaries of their current understanding, promoting a broader, more nuanced, or complex perspective. Prompts can include the following:

- I hadn't considered this angle before, but now I see . . .
- This deepens my thinking about . . .
- An additional insight I gained from this is . . .
- I used to think __, but now I'm considering . . .

Last, the challenge stage compels students to confront uncertainties, contradictions, or gaps in their understanding of new content, setting the stage for targeted inquiry and clarification. Here are some prompts:

- A question I have about this is . . .
- While I understand __, I'm unsure about . . .
- I'm struggling with the idea that . . .
- I'm curious about . . .

Incorporating thinking routines into the offline station challenges students to pause during their learning, think about their thinking, and engage in reflection. These routines are powerful tools because they promote these essential skills:

- **Self-monitoring:** Using the See, Think, Wonder regularly helps students become more aware of their cognitive processes and more adept at monitoring their understanding. This ongoing reflection helps them track their progress and adjust their approach.
- **Cognitive flexibility:** The Connect, Extend, Challenge routine encourages students to reassess their previous ideas, adapt to new information, and think more flexibly. This capacity to shift thinking as they learn is a core component of executive functioning.

### #3: Ongoing Self-Assessment:

Too often, assessment is seen solely as the teacher's responsibility. However, when students engage in regular self-assessment, they become more active participants in their learning. Encouraging students to reflect on and evaluate their work allows them to gain a deeper understanding of their strengths, limitations, and areas for improvement. This process helps shift ownership of learning from the teacher to the student, fostering a greater sense of responsibility for the quality of their work and their academic progress.

Self-assessment empowers students to do the following:
- **Monitor their progress:** Regular reflection helps students track their growth and adjust their strategies as they work toward specific learning goals.
- **Identify gaps in understanding:** Self-assessment encourages students to recognize where they may need additional support or clarification, allowing them to advocate for their needs.

Incorporating self-assessment with an exercise like the one pictured in figure 8.6 helps students take control of their learning journey, making them more aware, independent, and capable.

You can ask students to focus on a specific concept, skill, or behavior to self-assess, or you can give students the agency to select one they've been working on that week. The goal is to shift the responsibility for thinking about progress from teacher to learner, clarifying how students are doing and where they need to spend more effort working toward learning and behavior goals.

## Self-Assessment

| How do you feel like you are doing? | Agh. I'm not feeling good about this. | Not sure. I could use some help! | I've got this! I'm feeling good! | I feel GREAT! I'm ready for more. |
|---|---|---|---|---|
| [Assignment, skill, behavior] | | | | |
| [Assignment, skill, behavior] | | | | |
| [Assignment, skill, behavior] | | | | |

**Figure 8.6: Emoji Hands Self-Assessment Document**

## *After Learning: Reflection*

Reflection at the end of a lesson requires students to pause and consider what they learned, how they learned it, and what may still be unclear or confusing. Building a reflective practice in the classroom helps students to better understand the impact of learning on their thinking and skill set. It can also provide teachers with invaluable formative assessment data.

Reflection doesn't need to be complicated. You can use a simple 3-2-1 reflection, as shown in figure 8.7, asking students to identify three things they learned, two questions they have, and one connection they made.

| 3 Things You Learned | |
|---|---|
| 2 Questions You Have | |
| 1 Connection You Made | |

**Figure 8.7: 3-2-1 Reflection**

This simple exercise not only encourages students to consolidate and process new information, but it also fosters metacognitive awareness, prompting them to think about their learning process.

You can also use exit tickets, journal prompts, pair-share discussion questions, concept mapping, reflective role-playing activities, surveys, or self-evaluations with rubrics to get students to reflect on their learning. As discussed in the meaning-making section, providing students with a "would you rather" choice will make engaging in a reflective practice more accessible for all learners.

As we close this chapter, I want to acknowledge a common concern: Many teachers feel intimidated by the time and effort it may take to design lessons with the Station Rotation Model. However, teachers can streamline the design process by incorporating regular metacognitive routines and meaning-making activities. Once you establish a toolbox full of these strategies—whether it's a hands-on meaning-making task, reflection exercise, or goal-setting routine—you'll find that many of these activities can be adapted and reused throughout the school year, regardless of the content.

The beauty of this approach is that you're not reinventing the wheel every time you set up the offline station. Instead, you're drawing from a set of reliable, engaging activities that promote deeper thinking and self-regulation. Depending on where your students are in the learning cycle, you can easily pull from these resources to design your station. This not only saves time but also ensures that students are continually engaging in meaningful and reflective work that pushes them toward greater agency and independence in their learning.

## Summary

By prioritizing student agency in the offline station, teachers can encourage deeper meaning-making and reflection, helping students develop critical thinking and metacognitive skills. Teachers can streamline their design process by cultivating a toolkit of meaning-making and metacognitive activities. These can be reused and adapted throughout the year, making the offline station an essential, efficient, and dynamic component of the Station Rotation Model.

## Reflect and Discuss

1. How might prioritizing student agency at the offline station change the way students engage with learning activities? What are some specific ways you can offer students meaningful choices at this station?
2. Think about the types of meaning-making activities you currently use in your classroom. How could you expand these to better engage students in the process of interpreting, organizing, and understanding new information?
3. In what ways can metacognitive activities at the offline station help students strengthen their executive functioning skills, like setting goals, planning, staying organized, managing time, monitoring progress, and reflecting on learning? Describe the connection in your own words.
4. Designing stations can seem time intensive. How could developing a toolbox of meaning-making and metacognitive activities

streamline the planning process for the offline station? What are some activities you could add to your toolbox right now?

5. What challenges do you anticipate when incorporating these activities into your offline station? How might you overcome those challenges?

## Time to Apply: Design an Offline Learning Station

**Objective:** In this activity, you will design an offline learning station to engage students in either a meaning-making activity or a metacognitive routine. The goal is to create a station that fosters student agency and deeper learning through hands-on, reflective, and engaging tasks.

### Step 1: Identify the Learning Objective or Standard

Select a learning objective or standard for your offline station. What do you want students to learn, understand, or be able to do by the end of this station? Ensure that the task you design aligns with this goal and helps students engage deeply with the material.

### Step 2: Choose Your Focus

Decide whether your offline station will focus on a meaning-making activity or a metacognitive routine. If you choose a meaning-making activity, consider activities such as:

- Creating concept maps or diagrams to visualize ideas
- Building physical models or representations of key concepts
- Organizing information or materials in a way that deepens understanding (e.g., sorting, categorizing)
- Engaging in collaborative group work where students discuss and analyze content

If you choose a metacognitive routine, think about how you can help students reflect on their learning through:

- Goal-setting and revisiting their progress toward these goals
- Self-assessment prompts that ask students to evaluate their understanding
- Thinking routines like See, Think, Wonder and Connect, Extend, Challenge, where students think about how their understanding has evolved

## *Step 3: Design the Activity or Routine*

Once you've selected your focus, design the specific activity or routine for the station. Consider how it will encourage students to engage deeply with the content or reflect on their learning process:

- How does this task help students better understand the material or their own thinking?
- What steps will students take to complete the activity or routine?
- How will you introduce the task and guide students through it?

## *Step 4: Streamline Your Design Process*

Reflect on how you can reuse and adapt the activity or routine throughout the school year.

## *Step 5: Peer Feedback*

Share your station concept with a colleague and request feedback.

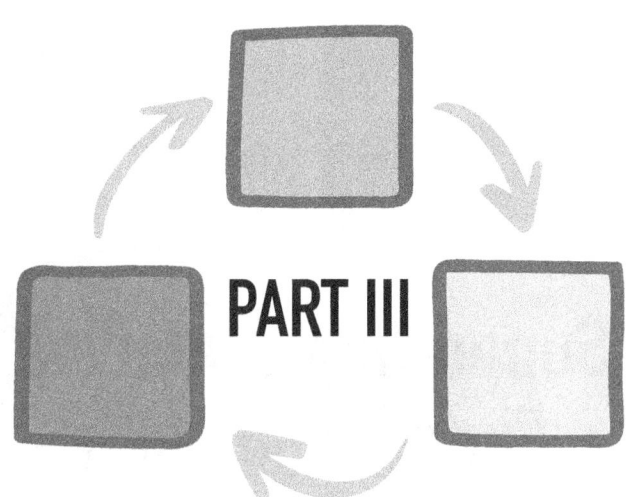

# PART III

# INNOVATING THE STATION ROTATION MODEL

CHAPTER 9

# Supporting Executive Functioning with Station Rotation

## Behaviors, Behaviors, Behaviors!

When I began my blog in 2009, I quickly realized that if I wanted anyone to read it or even find it, I also needed to have a presence on social media where I could share my work with a larger audience. Like all things, social media comes with benefits and challenges. I've had the pleasure of connecting with educators all over the world, exchanging ideas and learning from each other. I have also had people dismiss my ideas or criticize my work (often, I suspect, without even reading it). That comes with the territory, but it doesn't mean it doesn't sting.

I recently had an educator respond to one of my reels on Instagram, asking me if I'd ever spent any time in a classroom. She informed me that if I had any experience in a classroom, I would know that running small groups is a waste of time because it results in "behaviors, behaviors, behaviors." Oh my . . . There is so much to unpack here.

Her comment felt dismissive of my experience, but it also shined a light on a common misconception about student-directed learning models like the Station Rotation Model. Many assume that giving students more autonomy will lead to chaos or disengagement. However, my years in education have taught me that the success of any instructional approach—whether it's station rotation or project-based learning—depends on a foundation of strong classroom culture and clear expectations.

I've spent quite a lot of time in classrooms, both as a teacher and now as a coach and professional learning facilitator. I've been in every grade level and just about every subject-area classroom you can think of, including Latin, ceramics, dance, and esports game theory. I've worked with thousands of teachers, adapting the Station Rotation Model for their specific classes, and I've encountered almost every challenge a teacher can face in implementing a model that shifts control to students. The "behaviors" comment stung, but what bothered me more was the implication that students aren't capable of managing themselves or focusing on learning tasks without the teacher directing every aspect of the experience.

In reality, with the right scaffolding, a strong classroom culture, and focus on developing executive functioning skills, students can thrive in a more self-directed and collaborative learning environment. Shifting to the Station Rotation Model doesn't mean chaos; it means an opportunity to cultivate skills like self-regulation, emotional capacity, and strategic thinking. The challenge isn't in the model but in preparing students with the routines and support they need to navigate these learning experiences independently.

If we're kind, consistent, and transparent, we can help students develop essential skills like self-management, responsible decision-making, and time management—skills that will serve them long after they leave our classrooms.

## Firm Goals

By the end of this chapter, you will:

- Understand executive functioning skills and several methods for helping students cultivate them.
- Learn how to co-create class agreements and set clear expectations for behavior in a Station Rotation Model experience.
- Grasp the importance of creating a clear path of consequences and asking students to reflect on missteps in the classroom.

## Executive Functioning

When teachers transition from whole-group, teacher-led lessons to the Station Rotation Model, they release control over key elements of the learning experience to students, specifically the pace and path of student learning. At the student-led stations, learners can move more quickly or slowly through a learning task. They may also have control over their learning pathway, making choices about what they learn, how they learn, or what they create to demonstrate their learning. This shift in control positions students to take a more active role in their learning experiences, developing skills like self-regulation, time management, and decision-making.

The updated CAST framework weaves executive functioning through each of its guidelines, and the Station Rotation Model presents an excellent opportunity to address this focus by developing students' emotional capacity, their ability to build knowledge, and their strategic thinking as they navigate tasks independently and collaboratively with peers. Table 9.1 reviews these three dimensions of executive functioning and outlines how teachers can target the development of these skills as they use the Station Rotation Model.

## Table 9.1: Executive Functioning and the Station Rotation Model

| Executive Functioning Skills | Definition | Station Rotation Application | Example Station Activities |
|---|---|---|---|
| **Emotional capacity** | Students recognize and regulate emotions, manage thoughts and behaviors, and empathize with others. | Offer diverse, flexible learning experiences that allow for self-paced work, collaborative tasks, and reflection, helping students build awareness of their emotions and how to manage them in various situations. | • Reflection<br>• Emotional check-in<br>• Body scans<br>• Breathing exercises<br>• Feelings graph |
| **Knowledge-building** | Students actively transform information into usable knowledge by connecting new information to prior knowledge, synthesizing ideas, asking questions, and collaborating to co-construct understanding. | Offer stations where students can question, explore, discuss, and connect ideas. Collaborative stations encourage students to articulate their thinking, engage in inquiry, and share diverse perspectives, while individual stations can encourage reflection and independent meaning-making activities. | • Thinking routines, like See, Think, Wonder or Connect, Extend, Challenge<br>• Small-group discussions offline or asynchronous online discussions<br>• Collaborative research to build background<br>• Role-playing, debates, labs, experiments |

| **Strategic thinking** | Students set meaningful goals, planning for challenges, organizing resources, monitoring progress, and evaluate the effectiveness of specific strategies. | Offer multiple opportunities for students to practice strategy development, allowing them to set goals, plan steps, organize information, and reflect on their progress regularly. | • Goal-setting<br>• Self-assessment<br>• Planning document<br>• Identifying and curating resources |
|---|---|---|---|

Teachers looking to incorporate executive functioning skills can dedicate a station in each rotation to targeting the development of one of these aspects. For example, you may want to devote a station at the beginning of a unit to goal-setting and providing students with the time to think about what they care about and want to work toward—academically, personally, and/or behaviorally. Students can integrate self-assessment exercises, paired with reflections, to think critically about what they are learning about their strengths, limitations, growth, and areas of need.

You may also want to dedicate station time to activities designed to aid the development of knowledge-building and metacognition, like the collection of thinking routines developed by Project Zero at the Harvard Graduate School of Education.[1]

On my blog, my colleague Noelle Gutierrez describes a strategy she calls the relaxation station.[2] She outlines how she worked with a teacher to design a mini-playlist that students could work through at a station to prioritize their well-being, mental health, and emotional capacity. Noelle's station concept was so inspiring I designed an elementary and secondary version, as pictured in figures 9.1 and 9.2. These are designed to be self-paced station activities that allow students to explore strategies to help them more successfully regulate their emotions in and out of the classroom.

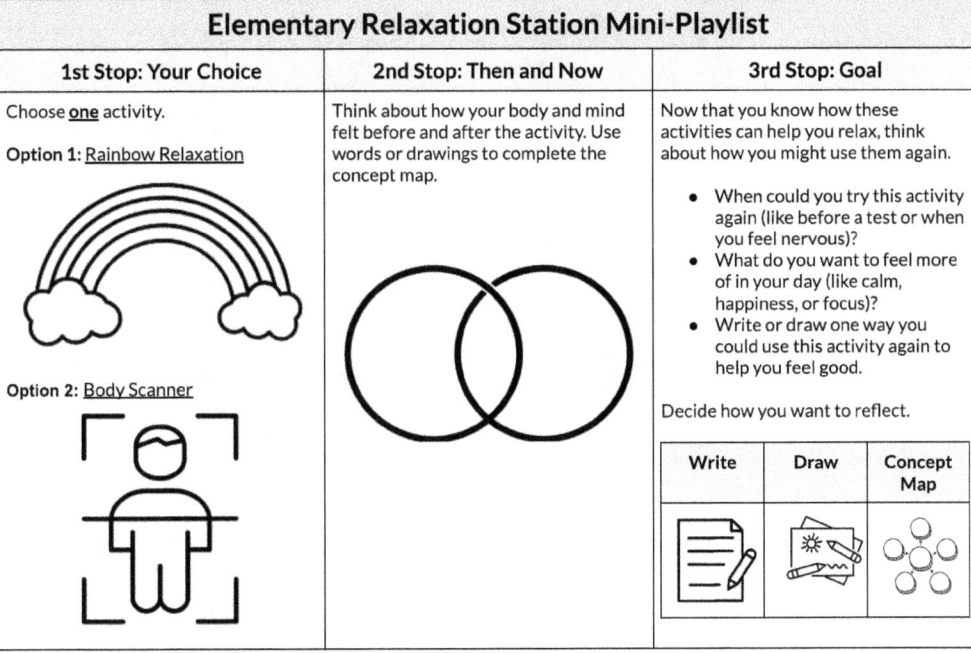

Figure 9.1: Elementary Relaxation Station Mini-Playlist

The secondary version of the relaxation station mini-playlist embeds structured opportunities for metacognition, reflection, and goal-setting—skills at the heart of executive functioning. Rather than simply guide students through a mindfulness activity, this revision invites them to make intentional choices, reflect on their mental and physical state before and after the experience, and set a meaningful well-being goal. Each step is designed to help students build self-awareness, monitor how strategies impact their emotional state, and apply those insights to their daily lives. By making time for this kind of student-centered reflection, the playlist empowers learners to take ownership of their emotional regulation and supports the development of sustainable habits that can extend beyond the classroom.

| Secondary Relaxation Station Mini-Playlist |||
| --- | --- | --- |
| Path | Directions | Work/Notes |
| Complete A Well-Being Activity | **Step 1:** Choose <u>one</u> of the following activities: a body scan or a belly breathing exercise.<br><br>**Step 2:** Put in your headphones and watch the video for your chosen activity to get a step-by-step guide through this activity.<br>    Option 1: **Body Scan**<br>    Option 2: **Belly Breathing** | **Explain Your Choice:** Which strategy are you choosing? Why? |
| Reflection: Your Body and Mind Before | Select <u>one</u> strategy from the **choice board** to guide your reflection. Consider the following questions as you reflect.<br>• How are you feeling before starting the exercise? (e.g., stressed, calm, energized)<br>• Is there anything on your mind distracting you?<br>• How is your body feeling (e.g., tired, sore, stiff)? | Share your reflection here. |
| Reflection: Your Body and Mind After | Select <u>one</u> strategy from the **choice board** to guide your reflection. Consider the following questions as you reflect.<br>• How are you feeling before starting the exercise (e.g., stressed, calm, energized)?<br>• What did you notice during the body scan or breathing exercise? Did certain parts of your body feel tense? Did you find it hard to focus on your breathing?<br>• Did any specific thoughts come to mind during the activity? How did you handle these thoughts?<br>• How do you think this exercise might help you in other situations (like before a test, when you're feeling stressed, or before bed)?<br>• Would you choose this activity again if you needed to relax or focus? Why or why not?<br>• Would you change anything to make this experience more effective for you? | Share your reflection here. |
| Set a Goal for Yourself | Now that you've taken a moment to practice mindfulness, you've given your mind and body a chance to reset and recharge. Think about how you might carry a little of that calm with you into your day. Let's set a small goal that supports your well-being.<br><br>• What is one simple goal you can set to support your mental or physical well-being in the coming days or weeks?<br>• Is there a small change you could make to bring more moments like this into your day?<br>• When could you practice this mindfulness strategy again, and how often would be realistic for you?<br>• What's one thing you'd like to feel more of (e.g., calm, focus, energy) or less of (e.g., stress, tension) in your daily life? How could this strategy help you? | **Your Goal:** What do you want to work toward?<br><br>**Your Plan:** How will you work toward this goal? What will you do? |

Figure 9.2: Secondary Relaxation Station Mini-Playlist

# Expectation-Setting for the Station Rotation Model

As students engage in tasks independently or collaboratively as part of the Station Rotation Model, they take more ownership of the learning process. For many students, the shift from teacher-centered to learner-centered lessons is huge and requires a completely new skill set. Weaving a focus on executive functioning into Station Rotation Model lessons can help students develop confidence in their ability to be successful in working through station tasks.

Developing student agency takes time, and students will be more successful if teachers provide clear modeling, scaffolding, and timely feedback. The transition to the Station Rotation Model will be smoother if you articulate the purpose behind the shift (the "why"), involve students in co-creating class agreements, establish clear consequences for behavior, and dedicate time for ongoing reflection.

## Step 1: Articulate the Why

In his book *Start with Why: How Great Leaders Inspire Everyone to Take Action*, Simon Sinek says, "We are drawn to leaders and organizations that are good at communicating what they believe. Their ability to make us feel like we belong, to make us feel special, safe and not alone is part of what gives them the ability to inspire us."[3] This is as true for teachers as it is for organizational leaders.

Teachers are leaders in their classrooms. They are responsible for creating a space where students feel safe, supported, and valued. Great teachers, like great leaders, inspire students by clearly communicating the "why" behind what they do. When teachers take the time to explain their instructional choices—whether transitioning to the Station Rotation Model, trying a new learning strategy, or integrating a technology tool—they demonstrate respect for their students as important members of the class community. It acknowledges that these instructional choices directly impact students, and we care enough to explain our motivation and reasoning to them. This reinforces the reality that teachers and students are partners in learning.

> *Great teachers, like great leaders, inspire students by clearly communicating the "why" behind what they do.*

When articulating the value of a shift from whole-group, teacher-led lessons to the Station Rotation Model, teachers can highlight the challenges of meeting everyone's needs with a single lesson. You can explain that the Station Rotation Model will create the time and space for you to work with small groups of students, ensuring the instruction, modeling sessions, support, and feedback meet their specific needs.

You can also acknowledge the reality that students acquire and process information and complete tasks at different rates, and the Station Rotation Model will give them a higher degree of control over the pace of their progress. Students are more likely to stay engaged and focused if they understand how a particular lesson design will benefit them, especially since blended learning models are more cognitively and socially demanding because they position students as active agents.

## Step 2: Co-Create Agreements

Rather than jump straight into the Station Rotation Model without establishing clear expectations, it's essential to engage students in a conversation about the behaviors and norms that will create a safe, respectful, and productive learning environment. Instead of simply providing a list of rules for students, co-creating agreements empowers learners to take ownership of the classroom culture and fosters a sense of shared responsibility.

The process of co-creating class agreements yields many benefits, such as:

- Clarity about expectations in a Station Rotation Model lesson
- Incorporation of students' prior experience in school
- Student conversations about academic behaviors and social interactions
- Collaboration as students work to define the actions and behaviors they think will keep interactions supportive, positive, and productive
- Student ownership of the process, which creates more buy-in to adhere to the norms and expectations

Gretchen Brion-Meisels, a lecturer at the Harvard Graduate School of Education, discusses the role of setting norms in creating "brave spaces," or classrooms "where students are encouraged to explore new ideas, respectfully challenge each other's assumptions, and make mistakes." Further, Brion-Meisels suggests, "Norms are a valuable way to help shape such a classroom culture."[4] Classrooms should be inclusive spaces where students feel safe taking risks, asking questions, acknowledging confusion, and failing forward. However, creating inclusive learning environments where students feel safe and supported requires intentionality. Cornell University's Center for Teaching Innovation describes inclusive learning communities as fostering "an environment where all students—regardless of their social identities, backgrounds, or beliefs—feel respected and valued." Additionally, this "forms a strong foundation for learning. It encourages an intellectual environment where a wide range of ideas and perspectives can be considered."[5] To create an inclusive learning community, we must create a classroom culture with clear expectations and also provide students with opportunities to get to know each other and work together.

The process I use when coaching teachers, pictured in table 9.2, anchors the creation of shared agreements in students' lived experiences, actively engages them in the process of generating norms, and encourages them to have conversations and collaborate with their classmates to identify the most important norms they want to add to a class list.

Table 9.2: Co-Creating Class Norms

| *Co-Creating Class Norms* |
|---|
| **Step 1: Ask students to reflect on their past experiences** |
| 1. Describe a learning environment that made you feel safe sharing ideas, engaging with classmates, and taking risks. What was it about that class or space that made you feel comfortable?<br>2. Next, describe a moment in school when you did not feel comfortable sharing your ideas, engaging with your classmates, or taking risks. What happened in those moments that made you feel unsafe or uncomfortable? |
| **Step 2: Give students time to identify key norms** |
| 1. Create small groups of three to four students.<br>2. Give them time to share and discuss their reflections about their past experiences in school.<br>3. Encourage them to identify three norms critical to creating and maintaining a safe learning environment.<br>4. Ask them to write their norms on paper or post them on a virtual Post-it note wall. |

| **Step 3: Facilitate a share-out and make a heat map** |
|---|
| 1. Ask one person from each group to share their three norms and briefly explain why these norms should be added to a class set of agreements.
2. Once all norms have been shared, give students time to review them (e.g., silent gallery walk).
    - If the norms are on poster paper or Post-it notes, make a heat map of dots to show interest.
    - If online, add a comment or heart their favorite norms.
3. Create a contract of five to ten agreements based on the norms that received the most dots or comments.
4. Finish by having students write the agreements on their syllabi or notebooks and ask them to sign them. |

After the class has created a list of agreements, these norms should be posted for easy reference, either in the classroom or online. For teachers with multiple classes, posting the agreements online can be especially helpful, as each class may have slightly different expectations. This ensures that students can easily access and revisit the agreements, reinforcing their ownership of the classroom norms.

## *Step 3: Establish a Clear Path of Consequences and Be Consistent*

Many classroom power struggles stem from unclear expectations and inconsistent consequences. This inconsistency can lead students to feel that consequences are unfair, which can, in turn, create said power struggles and strain teacher-student relationships. If there isn't a clear, established path of consequences for missteps, our responses to unproductive behaviors can vary depending on how we're feeling on a particular day. To maintain a safe and supportive learning environment, the best gift we can give our students is consistency in our expectations and responses.

When I was using the Station Rotation Model with students, I established the following path of consequences, described in table 9.3, for behaviors that violated our class agreements or distracted from the learning experience. The goal of this sequence is not to be overly punitive but to provide the student with a clear understanding of what will happen if they choose to violate an established expectation or agreement. Students can only make informed and responsible decisions if they know what the consequences of their actions are.

Table 9.3: Path of Consequences for Behaviors That Violate Class Agreements

| Path of Consequences for Behaviors That Violate Class Agreements | |
|---|---|
| Verbal warning | Give the student a verbal reminder about expected behavior. This gentle prompt gives the student a chance to correct their behavior before further action is taken. |
| A physical move | If the behavior persists, physically move the student to a different part of the classroom. This change in environment can help the student refocus without disrupting the rest of the class. |
| Safe space reflection | Ask the student to complete a Safe Space Reflection Form (see Table 9.4). This encourages the student to reflect on their behavior, identify the cause, and consider how they might improve moving forward. Before the student leaves class, have a conversation about the incident, using the form as a guide. |
| Conversation with the teacher | After reflection, have a one-on-one conversation with the student to discuss their behavior, the impact on the class, and strategies for improvement. This step focuses on guiding the student toward positive behavior choices. It also demonstrates that you care and want to work with the student to improve the situation. |
| Conversation with the family | If the behavior continues in a subsequent class, repeat the above steps and involve the student's family in the conversation. This helps to create a support system at home and at school, reinforcing the importance of behavior expectations and consequences. |
| Conversation with a counselor and/or administrator | For repeated or severe behavior issues, engage a counselor or administrator. This step emphasizes the seriousness of the behavior and engages additional support to address underlying issues and work toward positive changes. |

One key component of this path is the Safe Space Reflection Form, which is pictured in table 9.4. It offers students an opportunity to stretch their metacognitive muscles by encouraging them to pause, reflect on their behavior, and consider the impact of their choices. In completing a reflection form, students engage in self-assessment of their behavior and choices, exploring the reasons behind their actions and identifying strategies for improvement. This not only helps them develop self-awareness but also fosters a sense of accountability and personal growth.

The Safe Space Reflection Form can also help us to build empathy for our students. My experience is that the cause of unproductive behaviors usually has little to do with what is happening in the classroom; often, stressors outside of class are causing students to act out. When we understand what our students are metaphorically carrying into the classroom, we can better support them and connect them with resources that may be helpful.

**Table 9.4: Safe Space Reflection Form**

| Safe Space Reflection Form | |
|---|---|
| What happened? Describe the situation in your own words. | |
| Which of our class agreements did this behavior violate? | |
| Why did you do this? What motivated this behavior or caused you to act this way? | |
| How did your behavior impact me, your teacher? | |
| How did your behavior impact your classmates? | |
| How did your behavior impact you? | |
| If you find yourself in a similar situation in the future, how might you handle it differently? Can I support you in these moments? | |

If our goal is to support students in effectively regulating their emotions and engaging in productive, responsible ways, this path of consequences must be communicated clearly. Teachers might consider including language in their syllabi that explains each step and its purpose, emphasizing that this approach is meant to guide students in self-regulation and personal growth rather than simply punish misbehavior.

## Summary

It's essential when preparing for successful Station Rotation Model lessons to set the stage with intentionality, beginning with a focus on executive functioning. By proactively articulating the "why" behind our choices, we help students understand the purpose of their learning experience and their role in it. Co-creating agreements with students fosters a sense of ownership and community, and establishing a clear set of consequences ensures consistency and fairness in upholding expectations.

Simply by its nature, the Station Rotation Model will help students develop skills like self-regulation, time management, and strategic thinking. However, teachers can also regularly incorporate stations that target executive functioning skills through role-playing, discussion, relaxation, and well-being activities so that students engage with content and develop critical life skills. This approach empowers students to take greater responsibility for their learning, building a classroom culture where they can thrive.

## Reflect and Discuss

1. How would you describe your class culture? Is classroom management and student behavior a challenge?

2. To what extent are your students involved in co-creating classroom agreements? What benefits might arise from involving them more actively in this process?

3. How do you currently handle missteps and unproductive behavior in your class? How consistent are you in responding to unproductive behaviors? What impact does this have on your classroom culture?

4. Do your students understand the "why" behind the instructional strategies you're using? How might articulating the purpose of your approach impact their engagement and sense of responsibility?

5. How can you create a classroom culture that prioritizes both academic and social-emotional growth within the Station Rotation Model? How might focusing on executive functioning and creating a supportive classroom culture impact your students' ability to succeed both in your classroom and beyond?

6. What's one new strategy or approach from this chapter that you're excited to try in your classroom? How will you prepare students for this shift?

## Time to Apply: Create Your Own Executive Functioning Mini-Playlist

**Objective:** In this activity, you will design a mini-playlist for your students that allows them to self-pace through activities focused on building a specific executive functioning skill at a station. This playlist will support students in developing essential skills like self-regulation, time management, and strategic thinking while fostering independence and accountability.

### Step 1: Choose an Executive Functioning Focus

Decide which executive functioning skill you want to target with this mini-playlist. Reflect on your students' current strengths and areas for growth. Which executive functioning skill would benefit them most?

For example:

- Emotional capacity: Focus on self-awareness, emotional regulation, and empathy.
- Knowledge-building: Encourage active engagement, critical thinking, and making connections between concepts.
- Strategic thinking: Support goal-setting, planning, and adaptability in approaching tasks.

### Step 2: Create Short, Self-Contained Activities

Aim for two to three engaging activities within your students' scope of possibility, allowing them to work through the activities independently. Try to include a mix of tasks, such as individual reflection, practical application, and self-assessment. Reference table 9.1 (Executive Functioning and the Station Rotation Model) for activity ideas and inspiration.

### Step 3: Add Reflection Prompts to Build Metacognitive Skills

Include questions or prompts for each activity that encourage students to think about their thinking but provide them multiple pathways for sharing their reflections. This metacognitive practice will help them understand not only *what* they're learning but *how* they're learning.

### Step 4: Ask for Feedback

Share your mini-playlist with a colleague and request feedback or pilot your playlist with one class and ask your students for feedback on their experience. Then, make any necessary adjustments or revisions.

# CHAPTER 10

# Logistics and Setting the Stage for Station Rotation Success

## Orchestrating the Perfect Eightieth Birthday Dinner

As my dad approached his eightieth birthday, my sister and I decided to organize a dinner party at a nice restaurant near his home. I knew pulling the event off smoothly would require some serious planning. We had a larger group, so the restaurant insisted on family-style dining with a preset menu—three options for starters, mains, and dessert. As a vegetarian, I'm hyperaware of dietary restrictions, and as a mom, I've learned the hard way that people can have very strong (and unpredictable) feelings about food. So, I did my homework. I asked everyone ahead of time if there was anything they couldn't or wouldn't eat. No surprises meant everyone could enjoy their meal without any awkward moments of someone staring at a plate of food they weren't excited about.

Next came the seating arrangement. A sit-down dinner for a group this size needed more than a "just sit wherever" strategy. I made sure everyone had someone they knew nearby—because no one wants to feel stranded at a table—but I also wanted to mix things up enough to spark conversations among people who were not as close. My goal was for the stories about my dad's lifetime of antics and the accompanying laughter to flow all night, and a strategic seating arrangement helped make that happen. I also asked for a table outdoors on the heated patio, which is less crowded than the main dining room. I knew my parents, both of whom wear hearing aids, would have an easier time hearing conversations in a quieter setting.

Timing was another piece of the puzzle. My sister and I had a few heartfelt moments planned to honor my dad, but I didn't want the speeches or our surprise gift to compete with the sound of clinking glasses or waitstaff clearing plates. So, I worked with the restaurant to time those moments between courses, giving my dad the spotlight and pausing the meal to minimize distractions at key points.

All that planning paid off! The night flowed seamlessly, and we got to do all the celebratory things we wanted without a single hiccup. A little intentional planning about the menu, seating arrangement, location, and schedule went a long way. The same is true for station rotation in the classroom. Whether it's thinking through seating, timing transitions, or anticipating needs, the effort you put into preparing your lesson ensures a smoother experience for everyone involved. And just like that dinner party, when it all comes together, the results are worth it.

## Firm Goals

By the end of this chapter, you will:

- Understand how to group students flexibly for a variety of purposes.

- Appreciate the impact of furniture arrangement on focus and engagement.
- Grasp the importance of a clear and practiced transition strategy.
- Learn how to design tasks to keep fast finishers engaged.

## Flexible Grouping Strategies

The way we group students as part of the Station Rotation Model has a profound impact on their learning experience, particularly in the teacher-led station, where small-group instruction is designed to be differentiated to meet the diverse skills, abilities, and needs in a classroom. Flexible grouping allows you to tailor your approach to align with the specific learning objectives of the lesson, the data you've collected about your students, and the type of learning experience you want to create.

While grouping students is essential for effective teaching, it must be done thoughtfully to ensure no student feels marginalized or limited. Research underscores that grouping should never harm students by segregating them into fixed, low-ability tracks or isolating those with learning, behavioral, or emotional challenges. Instead, grouping should promote feelings of competence, self-determination, and positive connections with peers while fostering essential skills like personal responsibility, social-emotional growth, and self-directed learning.[1]

I've walked into a lot of classrooms that have groups written on the whiteboard in colored marker. There are the blue, purple, green, red, and orange groups. It doesn't take long for the students in the lower-ability group to understand why they've been grouped that way. My concern is that if students are put in skill-level groups and left there, it will have a negative impact on their perception of themselves and their potential as learners. That's why we need to think about the learning objective, the needs of our students, and the strategies we plan to use in our teacher-led station, then group our students strategically.

Table 10.1 displays several flexible grouping strategies teachers can use.

**Table 10.1: Grouping Strategies**

| Grouping Strategy | What Is It? | Example |
|---|---|---|
| **Mixed skill-level** | Students with diverse abilities are grouped together to foster peer learning. | Students with diverse abilities are grouped to tackle a math problem so stronger problem-solvers can model strategies for their peers. |
| **Skill or ability** | Students are grouped by similar skill levels for targeted instruction and support. | Students are grouped by reading level for a specific lesson focused on foundational reading skills or comprehension strategies, with groups changing as students progress. |
| **Needs-based** | Groups are formed based on immediate instructional needs or gaps identified by assessment data. Each group may receive totally different instruction. | Students are grouped based on formative assessment data to target a specific instructional need, such as organizing ideas or using evidence effectively when writing. |
| **Interest-based** | Students are grouped according to their interests or chosen topics. | Students select a short story to read and analyze, working in groups based on their shared interest in a particular story to deepen their understanding and engagement. |
| **Strengths in a group dynamic** | Groups are organized to balance complementary strengths for a shared task. | Students are grouped to balance diverse strengths, such as leadership, creativity, and organization, to create a shared project or presentation collaboratively. |

| Random | Students are grouped without any predetermined criteria. | A teacher uses a random name generator to assign groups for review activities, ensuring students work with various peers and build connections. |

Beyond the choice of grouping strategy, effective grouping also requires intentional effort to teach students how to work well together. You must take time to build the interpersonal and collaborative skills necessary for students to thrive in groups, as well as create an environment where all students feel valued and supported. Providing adequate resources—such as space, materials, and additional support—can further enhance the success of small groups by enabling a variety of cooperative learning activities.

Ultimately, grouping strategies should be a tool for empowering students, not labeling them. When students are flexibly and regularly regrouped based on their interests, needs, and the benefits of diversity, small learning groups can promote both academic achievement and a healthy classroom culture. By varying how students are grouped, and aligning decisions with clear learning objectives, we can create classrooms where every student has an opportunity to participate, contribute, and thrive.

> *Ultimately, grouping strategies should be a tool for empowering students, not labeling them.*

Once you have a clear grouping strategy in mind, you'll want to think about how to get students into their groups quickly. Projecting a visual display of groups, as pictured in figure 10.1, can help students quickly find their seats as they enter the classroom. This minimizes the time needed to transition into the stations.

| Station #1: Teacher-Led | Station #2: Online |
|---|---|
| 1. <br> 2. <br> 3. <br> 4. <br> 5. <br> 6. | 1. <br> 2. <br> 3. <br> 4. <br> 5. <br> 6. |
| **Station #3: Offline** | **Station #4: Would You Rather...?** |
| 1. <br> 2. <br> 3. <br> 4. <br> 5. <br> 6. | 1. <br> 2. <br> 3. <br> 4. <br> 5. <br> 6. |

**Figure 10.1: Station Rotation Grouping Display**

In addition to eliminating unnecessary transition time, you can use this visual display to indicate what number a student is assigned at each station, which allows you to set an intentional seating arrangement. Teachers often use seating charts during whole-group instruction to create a focused and productive learning environment. By considering factors like skill levels, behavior, personality, and strengths, you can strategically assign seats to foster engagement, improve focus, and encourage respectful interactions. When transitioning to the Station Rotation Model, the same intentionality can be applied to minimize unproductive and off-task behaviors.

Using various grouping strategies—such as skill level, interests, or group dynamics—allows teachers to align the seating arrangement with the purpose of the station. In classrooms where additional structure is needed, assigning seats and strategically grouping students can keep rotations running smoothly. This approach supports engagement and focus across the classroom and enables the teacher to concentrate fully on their work with small groups at the teacher-led station.

# Strategic Furniture Arrangement

As educators, we know the physical layout of a classroom profoundly influences how students engage with their learning and each other. Everything from lighting to temperature to furniture placement can support or hinder a student's focus and comfort.

Studies have consistently highlighted the connection between classroom layout, student behavior, and learning outcomes.[2] By intentionally arranging furniture, we can create a learning environment that fosters collaboration, active engagement, or quiet independent work—depending on what a given task requires. And while many teachers may not have access to flexible furniture or modern seating options, even the most basic setups can be adapted. Single desks, two-seater tables, and yes, even those all-too-familiar desks with chairs attached can be creatively rearranged to suit different activities. Teaching, after all, is often a series of "make it work" moments.

When I work with teachers implementing the Station Rotation Model, we discuss how classroom furniture sends subtle but powerful messages about the type of work students are expected to do.[3] For example, arranging desks so students face each other may unintentionally encourage conversation during tasks that require focus and concentration. A simple shift in furniture placement to a row of side-by-side desks can align the physical space with the cognitive demands of the activity, supporting both the teacher's goals and the student's success.

There are three main types of engagement that happen in each station, and the desired level of engagement should drive our decisions about how we lay out the furniture, as described in table 10.2.

## Table 10.2: Types of Engagement and the Furniture Arrangements That Work Best

| Type of Engagement | Description | Recommended Furniture Arrangement | Why It Works |
|---|---|---|---|
| Collaborative engagement | Students work together to solve problems, share ideas, or complete tasks. | Table groups: Students face each other. | It encourages communication, teamwork, and shared resources, fostering collaboration and interpersonal skills. |
| Individual engagement | Students work independently to complete assignments, reflect, or focus on tasks. | Rows or individual desks: Students face forward or face a wall. | It minimizes distractions, supports quiet concentration, and aligns with tasks requiring focus and privacy. |
| Teacher-led engagement | Students receive differentiated instruction, feedback, and support, and they engage in discussion. | U-shaped desk arrangement: Students face the teacher and whiteboard or screen. | It allows for clear visual access to teaching aids and easy interaction between the teacher and all students. |

The furniture arrangement should act as a silent partner in the learning process, supporting both the task and the desired learning outcomes.

## U-Shaped Desks for Teacher-Led Stations

When facilitating small-group instruction at the teacher-led station, a U-shaped desk arrangement, as pictured in figure 10.2, is particularly effective. This setup positions all students to face the teacher, fostering focus and direct engagement. The open layout allows the teacher to move easily within the group, providing targeted instruction, guidance, feedback, and support.

The U-shaped seating arrangement offers clear visual access to the whiteboard or other teaching aids, which can be invaluable for differentiated small-group lessons. Teachers can use the whiteboard to demonstrate key concepts, model problem-solving strategies, or display visuals to enhance understanding.

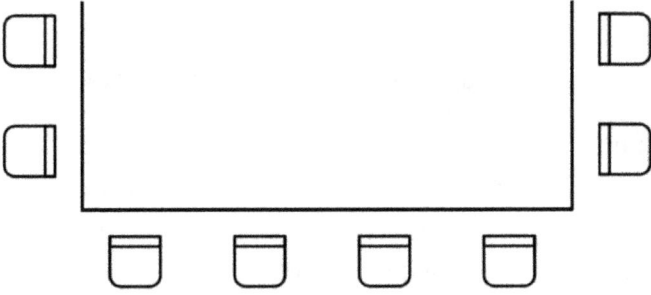

**Figure 10.2: U-Shaped Teacher-Led Station**

For teachers leveraging small-group time to facilitate discussions, the U-shaped arrangement also encourages participation and eye contact among students. This layout creates a more intimate environment, building community and promoting positive group dynamics. Whether explaining a challenging concept or guiding a collaborative conversation, teachers can use this seating arrangement to support academic and social objectives.

## Rows for Independent Tasks

While collaborative seating arrangements are effective for group work, independent tasks require a different setup to maximize focus and minimize distractions. Arranging desks in rows or straight lines, as pictured in figure 10.3, gives students a quieter, more structured environment where they can work individually without the temptation to interact with peers.

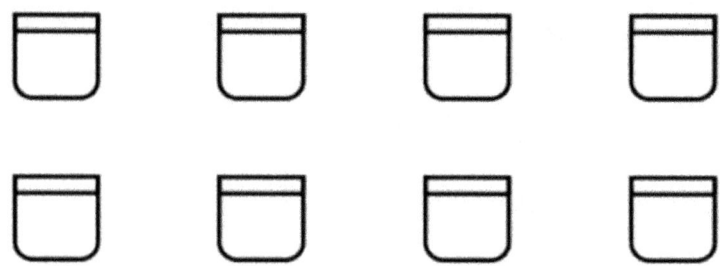

**Figure 10.3: Rows for Independent Work**

Positioning desks so students face away from the teacher-led station (during online or computer-based tasks) enables teachers to monitor their screens at a glance. This ensures students remain on task while preserving the independent nature of their work.

Rows also reinforce the expectation of quiet, focused effort, making it easier for students to concentrate on their learning activities. Whether students are completing a digital exercise, reading, or engaging in written reflection, the seating arrangement should support their need for privacy and focus.

## Table Groups for Collaboration

Collaboration thrives in a table-group setup, as pictured in figure 10.4. This arrangement supports peer-to-peer interactions, making it ideal for tasks that require discussion, problem-solving, and work on shared tasks. Students can exchange ideas, ask questions, and build on each other's contributions, leading to deeper learning and creative solutions.

# Logistics and Setting the Stage for Station Rotation Success

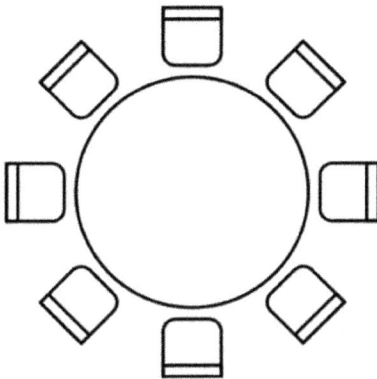

**Figure 10.4: Table Groups for Collaborative Tasks or Discussion**

Working in groups also develops essential social and interpersonal skills. Regular interaction fosters relationships, builds trust, and creates a sense of belonging within the classroom. As students collaborate, they practice taking on roles, such as facilitator, note-taker, or timekeeper, honing leadership and communication skills that will serve them well beyond the classroom.

Group seating arrangements encourage active participation and the exchange of ideas, empowering students to work together toward a common goal. The physical layout signals that collaboration is expected and valued, reinforcing the importance of teamwork in the learning process.

Thoughtfully arranging furniture can transform a classroom into an environment that enhances focus, encourages self-directed learning, and improves engagement. By aligning the physical setup with students' needs and learning objectives, you can create a space that sets the stage for meaningful learning and positive outcomes. If rearranging furniture feels overwhelming, consider involving your students—they'll appreciate the chance to help shape their learning environment!

# Decide on a Transition Strategy (and Practice, Practice, Practice!)

Transitions can either enhance or disrupt the flow of a lesson, so it's essential to design and practice them intentionally. When we ask students to transition from one station or learning activity to another, we expect a lot from our learners. They must wrap up what they are currently working on, even if they are not finished, gather and organize their belongings, and physically move from one location in the classroom to another. Given these demands, we must have a clear and consistent transition process that minimizes chaos and lost instructional time while maintaining a well-managed classroom.

I remember going into a third-grade class to support a teacher implementing the Station Rotation Model and encountering a particularly effective transition process. When the timer dinged to signal the end of the station, the teacher followed a three-step process to transition his students from one station to the next. He said, "One. Wrap up and clean up." The whole class began wrapping up their work and tidying up their stations, putting the supplies back in the buckets in the center of the tables. He gave them about thirty seconds and said, "Two. When you're ready, stand behind your chair with your things." As students became ready, they stood up, pushed in their chairs, and patiently stood behind them. It was fascinating to watch how this simple practice applied gentle visual pressure on the students who were taking a little longer to get their things packed up. The teacher did not have to verbally hurry them up. Finally, when everyone was standing quietly behind their chairs, the teacher said, "Three. Walk to the next station." In less than thirty seconds, the entire class was settled at their next station.

As I watched this transition seamlessly unfold, I realized I had done a terrible job of "training" my high school classes to transition effectively. I had assumed that teenagers did not need to practice a transition strategy. I was wrong! It doesn't matter what age our students are; we need a clear transition strategy, and we need to practice it until they can execute it seamlessly.

Table 10.3 identifies the key components teachers must consider when it comes to transitions.

**Table 10.3: The Components of a Seamless Transition**

| Components | What Is It? | Examples |
|---|---|---|
| **Projected timer** | During each station, display a timer that students can see to help them self-pace through a task and manage their time more effectively. | A physical timer in the room<br><br>A video timer displayed in a projected slide deck |
| **A clear signal to end the station** | End each rotation with a clear and consistent signal, alerting students that it's time to wrap up their current task. | Timer<br><br>Chime<br><br>Music<br><br>Verbal cue |
| **An explicit set of steps** | Provide students with clear, sequential instructions to guide the transition. | Step 1: Wrap up and clean up.<br><br>Step 2: Stand behind your chair quietly when you are ready to transition.<br><br>Step 3: Walk to the next station. |
| **Move from one station to the next** | Establish a clear "flow" for movement in the room, such as a clockwise or counterclockwise rotation. | Designated pathways<br><br>Tape arrows on the floor<br><br>Assigned seating<br><br>Numbers or colors to mark stations |

# Onboarding Students to the Transition Strategy

It doesn't matter how old students are; it is important to explicitly teach them how to transition from one station to another. Below are the steps I recommend when onboarding students to the transition strategy:

1. **Model the process.** Take time to model each part of the transition process explicitly. Demonstrate how to clean up quickly and efficiently, where to stand, and how to move quietly to the next station.
2. **Practice until the transition routine becomes automatic.** Transitions, like any classroom routine, require repetition. Practice with your students until they can execute the steps without hesitation.
3. **Provide positive reinforcement.** When students nail the transition, recognize and celebrate them.
4. **Transfer ownership of the process.** As students become more comfortable with the process, consider giving them ownership. For example, assign a "transition leader" to give verbal cues, set the timer, track how quickly the class transitions, and provide positive feedback.

Combining the components of effective transitions with an onboarding process can help teachers keep students focused, minimizing disruption and lost time. No matter the age of students, a clear and consistent transition routine is an essential aspect of maintaining effective classroom management when using the Station Rotation Model.

# Fast Finishers: What Next?

A benefit of the Station Rotation Model is that it gives students the opportunity to control the pace of their progress through learning activities (at the stations that are not teacher led).

Even though control over pacing is a benefit of the Station Rotation Model, many teachers worry about students finishing the work at a station before it's time to transition. They're afraid that if students are done with their work, they will distract or disrupt other students who are still working. I caution teachers not to jam stations so full of work that students are unable to finish the tasks they are assigned. Instead, recognize that students will work through tasks at different rates, and some will finish before others. The best way to handle that is to have a next-steps protocol or a may-do list for students to work on. See table 10.4. for examples.

**Table 10.4: Strategies for Fast Finishers**

| Next-Steps Protocol | May-Do List |
|---|---|
| Continue working on any unfinished assignments from a previous station. | Read your independent reading book. |
| Check your work and make any necessary revisions. | Study for the upcoming quiz. |
| | Complete a brain break activity. |
| Grab a student tutor lanyard and help students who need additional support at the other stations. | Spend time practicing a mindfulness activity. |
| Work on the challenge/extension activity. | |

Teachers can also create a "brain break choice board" like the one pictured in figure 10.5. When students are done with a task, they can choose a relaxing activity to engage with. It can be helpful to have baskets of supplies in a designated location that students can grab if they have time to complete a brain break activity.

## The Station Rotation Model and UDL

| Brain Break Choice Board |||
|---|---|---|
| *If you are finished at your station and do not need to return to a previous station to finish a task, select an activity from the board below to work on!* |||
| Color or Draw | Make Progress on Our Puzzle | Create Blackout Poetry |
| Read for Pleasure | Listen to Music or a Podcast | Build Something |

Figure 10.5: Brain Break Choice Board

# Station Rotation Checklists: Reinforce Student Ownership

Teachers often feel pressure to assign a deliverable—a product that students submit at the end of each station to keep them on task and accountable for completing the work assigned. Unfortunately, the result is an unsustainable amount of work for teachers. If you feel obligated to collect and grade work from every station, the resulting workload will quickly overshadow the Station Rotation Model's benefits, making it unsustainable.

Instead of relying on deliverables, you can use a checklist, like the one shown in table 10.5, to shift the responsibility for monitoring learning to your students. By incorporating metacognitive tasks into these checklists, you can encourage *students* to think about their thinking, reflect on their learning process, and track their progress.

This approach not only reduces the grading burden, but it also shifts the focus to metacognitive skill-building, fostering critical thinking, self-awareness, and independence in students.[4] Ultimately, it shifts the focus of the Station Rotation Model from task completion to meaningful engagement and learning.

Table 10.5: Station Rotation Lesson Checklist

| | Station Rotation Lesson Checklist | |
|---|---|---|
| **Teacher-led station** | Complete the 3-2-1 reflection before leaving this station. | |
| | 3 things you learned | 1. <br><br> 2. <br><br> 3. |
| | 2 questions you have | 1. <br><br> 2. |
| | 1 thing that surprised you | 1. |
| **Online station** | Complete the Connect, Extend, Challenge thinking routine.<br>• How did what you learned at this station **connect** to what you already knew?<br>• How did what you learned at this station **extend** your thinking about this topic?<br>• What was **challenging** or confusing? What are you wondering about? | |

| | |
|---|---|
| **Offline station** | Take a moment to think about how you engaged at this station and complete the self-assessment below.<br><br>**Beginning:** I did not participate actively in discussion or collaboration.<br><br>**Developing:** I participated in the discussion or collaboration and made some attempts to ask questions, build on ideas shared, or make connections.<br><br>**Proficient:** I consistently participated in discussions or collaboration, asking questions, building on ideas shared, offering suggestions, and making connections.<br><br>**Mastery:** I took on a leadership role in the discussion or collaboration, inviting quieter students to contribute, helping to guide the conversation, and working to ensure everyone was included.<br><br>**Reflection:**<br>• What level of mastery did you display today?<br>• Why did you give yourself this score?<br>• What do you want to improve on next time? |
| **"Would you rather" station** | Think about the choice you made at this station and reflect.<br>• Which choice did you make and why?<br>• Was this the best choice for you now that you've completed this task?<br>• Would you make the same decision if you were offered this choice again? |

Station rotation checklists are also a powerful tool for gathering valuable formative assessment data without increasing your workload. These checklists can include tasks that provide insight into students' understanding of key concepts or ability to apply specific skills in a low-stakes format. For example, students might be asked to create an analogy demonstrating their grasp of a concept, solve a problem that applies a newly learned strategy, or write a one-sentence summary of what they learned. These quick, targeted tasks not only help students reflect on their learning, but they also give you meaningful data to identify students who may need additional instruction or support and those who are ready for a next-level challenge.

In addition to individual tasks, checklists can prompt students to assess their confidence in applying a skill or understanding a concept. Questions like "How confident are you in your ability to explain this to a peer?" or "What part of this task was most challenging for you?" can provide valuable insights into where students might need additional support. Over time, this data allows you to adjust instruction, tailor small-group lessons, and ensure students are making progress toward their goals.

Checklists also serve as valuable documentation of student engagement and progress within stations. If a student consistently fails to complete items on the checklist, it provides an opportunity for the teacher to have a meaningful conversation to uncover potential barriers and address them. This documentation can also be a helpful reference during discussions with families about a student's performance and growth.

## Summary

Effective use of the Station Rotation Model begins with intentional design that fosters focus, engagement, and collaboration. Thoughtful furniture arrangements and flexible grouping strategies enable students to work productively on various activities, from independent tasks to collaborative challenges. Clear and consistent transitions minimize chaos and lost time, ensuring smooth movement between stations. To reduce teacher workload and deepen student learning, metacognitive checklists can replace deliverables, shifting accountability and ownership to students. These checklists also provide valuable formative data to inform future instruction, supporting differentiation and personalization. By combining purposeful design with structured routines, we can create a dynamic, student-centered learning environment and a sustainable approach to the Station Rotation Model.

## Reflect and Discuss

1. How does the current furniture layout in your classroom support or distract from the types of engagement you want to see during station rotations? What adjustments might you make after reading the suggestions in this chapter? If the furniture arrangement needs to change, how can you engage your students in this process?

2. What grouping strategies do you typically use? How might grouping and regrouping students flexibly with various strategies (e.g., interest-based or mixed-ability groups) improve student engagement and learning?

3. What are the biggest challenges you face during transitions? What strategies from this chapter could help minimize chaos and maximize instructional time?

4. How do you currently teach and reinforce expectations for smooth transitions? How might you refine or practice these routines with your students?

5. How do you hold students accountable for their work during stations? What challenges do you face with this approach? How could implementing checklists with metacognitive tasks shift accountability to students while reducing your workload?

6. How do you encourage students to take ownership of their learning during stations? What steps can you take to scaffold metacognitive practices (such as reflecting on effort, progress, or next steps) for your students?

## Time to Apply: Design a Metacognitive Checklist

**Objective:** In this chapter, we explored how replacing station deliverables with metacognitive checklists can shift accountability to students while providing teachers with valuable formative assessment data. Now, it's your turn to put this into practice by designing a metacognitive checklist for a Station Rotation Model lesson you plan to implement.

### Step 1: Identify Learning Goals

What are the key skills, concepts, or outcomes students should focus on in each station? How can reflection help students connect to these goals and monitor their progress?

### Step 2: Plan Reflection Prompts for Each Station

For each station (e.g., teacher-led, online, offline), design two to three reflection prompts or self-assessment questions.

Consider including tasks that encourage students to:
- Summarize what they learned, putting it in their own words
- Evaluate their effort or engagement
- Identify challenges or ask questions
- Set a goal for improvement

### Step 3: Keep It Age Appropriate

Keep the following considerations in mind:
- Use clear and simple language for prompts to ensure students understand the task.
- Incorporate visuals or scales (e.g., emojis, stars) for younger students to make self-assessment engaging and accessible.

### Step 4: Make It Actionable

Think about the following points when designing your checklist:

- Structure the checklist so it provides useful insights into student progress.
- Consider how you'll use the information to adjust instruction or provide feedback.

**CHAPTER 11**

# Creative Alternatives to the Traditional Station Rotation

## From Meal Service to Master Chef

When my kids turned thirteen and fifteen, I decided it was time for them to learn to cook. Cooking is an essential life skill, and as teenagers, they didn't fully appreciate the time and effort that goes into preparing meals. To make it fun and manageable, I signed up for Green Chef, a meal service, and tasked each of them with choosing and cooking one meal a week.

The meal service provided the perfect starting point. It offered them agency—they got to pick meals they were excited to prepare—and gave them the scaffolds they needed. Each meal came with premeasured ingredients and step-by-step instructions, complete with photos. They didn't have to worry about where to start or how to finish; they just had to follow the plan.

At first, the goal was simple: Teach them basic cooking skills while helping them appreciate the effort that goes into making a meal. But what started as a structured, guided experience turned into something far more meaningful, especially for my daughter.

Fast-forward a few years, and at seventeen, she's now a talented and adventurous cook. Her journey didn't stop with the meal service recipes. She started following food creators on Instagram, learning from chefs and bakers who shared innovative dishes. She experimented with everything from intricate cookie recipes to sweet dumplings to homemade pasta. This past holiday season, she took over the kitchen, preparing homemade rosemary mashed potatoes, a decadent baked macaroni and cheese inspired by an Instagram post, and even a glazed Christmas ham, despite being a vegetarian.

Her confidence and creativity in the kitchen are incredible to watch. She's moved far beyond the simple, scripted recipes of those early days, challenging herself with intricate and unusual dishes. Cooking is no longer just a life skill for her; it's a passion she continues to explore and refine.

The evolution from those first preplanned meals to creating her own culinary masterpieces is the perfect metaphor for how a structured, guided beginning can blossom into something so much more. Similarly, the Station Rotation Model has many exciting variations that teachers can play with once they're comfortable applying the base design to their lessons. In this chapter, we'll explore some of the ways teachers can modify the classic Station Rotation Model to create more opportunities for students to control the pace and path of their experience while freeing the teacher to provide more targeted and personalized support.

## Firm Goals

By the end of this chapter, you will:

- Be able to modify the classic design of the Station Rotation Model to provide students with more control over the pace and path of their learning.

- Understand how a rotation can be used to provide students with additional instruction and support tailored to their specific needs.

# Thinking Outside the Box with the Station Rotation Model

The Station Rotation Model is a flexible instructional approach with endless possibilities in terms of design. As you become more comfortable and confident designing lessons with it, I suggest exploring variations that leverage the rotation design for a variety of different purposes. Just one tool does not work to solve all problems. In that light, the traditional Station Rotation Model design may not be the best fit for all lessons or lesson objectives. In this chapter, we will explore a few variations that shift more control over the learning experience to the students.

## Variation #1: Free-Flow, Student-Paced Station Rotation

One of my favorite variations on the traditional Station Rotation Model is the free-flow, student-paced rotation, which puts students in control of their progress through the learning activities. Instead of feeling rushed because they're trying to complete a task on a teacher-dictated timeline, or bored because they're done and waiting to transition, students move between stations when *they* are ready.

How does this variation work? Just like in the traditional Station Rotation Model, students begin at a specific station at the start of the lesson. But instead of relying on the teacher to determine the amount of time they spend at each station, students transition when they complete the task at their current station. This allows learners to spend more time on tasks that require deeper focus, more processing time, or additional effort while moving more quickly through tasks they find easier.

To ensure the free-flow, student-paced model runs smoothly, teachers should:

- **Establish clear expectations:** Make sure students know what they need to accomplish at each station before they transition to the next station. Using a checklist, as described in chapter 10, can help keep students focused and on track during a free-flow rotation.
- **Create a clear question protocol:** Ask students to do something simple like put a colorful Post-it on their computer or a corner of their desk to signal that they have a question. Older students can write their question on a Post-it and put it on a designated spot on the front board (if you're busy providing feedback or working with another student or small group).
- **Be flexible:** Remember that students will be progressing at different rates, so it's important to design stations that don't require students to be in sync with one another. Communication or collaboration will need to be asynchronous (e.g., via online discussions or a virtual Post-it note wall).

When should a teacher consider using a free-flow, student-paced Station Rotation Model? The two factors you must consider are the time required to complete the learning activities and how you want to use your time during the rotation.

This approach works best when the learning activities are likely to take variable time, with some students needing significantly more or less time for completion. Table 11.1 lists a few such activities.

**Table 11.1: Learning Activities That Benefit from Self-Pacing**

| Learning Activities That Benefit from Self-Pacing | |
|---|---|
| **English language arts** | Writing assignments |
| | Actively reading a complex text |
| **Math** | Solving a series of increasingly complex problems |
| | Real-world application activities |
| **Science** | Conducting a lab or experiment |
| | Analyzing and interpreting data |
| **History or social science** | Research projects |
| | Reading and analyzing primary or secondary sources |
| **Art and design** | Creating physical or digital artwork |
| | Building a portfolio of work |
| **World languages** | Writing assignments |
| | Reading or listening and completing a comprehension task |
| **Physical education** | Completing a fitness challenge |
| | Researching and writing about a specific sport or aspect of health and nutrition |

The free-flow, student-paced approach is *not* ideal if you intend to provide differentiated instructional sessions. For example, if you plan to model a skill or deliver instruction using strategies like "I do, we do, pairs do, you do," hook the group, or concept attainment (as covered in chapter 6), then remember that these activities require a set amount of uninterrupted instructional time. Having students join the teacher-led station midway through an explanation because they finished the previous station would be disruptive.

Instead, this student-paced version works best when the teacher-led station involves providing real-time feedback or pulling individual students or small groups for Tier 2 or Tier 3 interventions. If you're providing students with real-time formative feedback, then they can join the teacher-led station at any time and leave once they have received their feedback and made the necessary edits. If you need to provide Tier 2 or Tier 3 interventions, you can even pull students from the free-flow rotation for that instruction and support.

The free-flow, student-paced station rotation is especially valuable because it meets students' psychological need for autonomy. It can positively impact their feelings of competence because it allows them to be more in control of their experience. It can also give you time to provide personalized feedback, instructional support, or interventions.

## Variation #2: Must-Do vs. May-Do Station Rotation

Classrooms are composed of diverse groups of students. Given that variability, not all students need to spend time engaged in the same learning tasks or activities. As you gain confidence with the Station Rotation Model, you can experiment with a fun variation of the traditional design of a rotation that consists of must-do and may-do learning activities.

In a traditional Station Rotation Model, all students rotate through the same sequence of learning activities, or stations. By contrast, the must-do vs. may-do variation does not require that students go to every station. This twist combines data-informed design with an emphasis on student agency to create a more personalized and student-centered approach to the Station Rotation Model.

How does the must-do vs. may-do variation work? Like a traditional Station Rotation Model, determine a set time for each rotation (e.g., twenty to thirty minutes) and cue transitions. Assign one or two must-do stations tailored to each student's needs. Let students know that after completing these required stations, they can choose from may-do stations based on their preferences and interests.

To maximize the effectiveness of this model, you should dedicate your teacher-led station to high-need instructional tasks. For example, in a rotation with four stations, you can use the teacher-led station in each rotation to provide targeted instruction or support on a different concept or skill that several students struggle with. Over the course of the four stations, you can provide explicit instruction on four different areas of need, requiring specific students to attend the teacher-led instructional sessions in those areas. You can also use this station for Tier 2 or Tier 3 interventions, offering intensive, small-group support for students requiring additional help with specific skills or concepts.

By strategically using the teacher-led station for high-impact instructional tasks, you ensure students receive the personalized support they need while maintaining the flexibility and agency that make the must-do vs. may-do model so powerful.

To ensure this variation runs smoothly:

- **Clarify the purpose and structure:** Explain the purpose of the must-do vs. may-do structure, emphasizing its benefits (e.g., targeting individual learning needs while offering students choice). Clearly outline how many stations students are expected to attend, highlighting which are mandatory. Visual aids, such as charts or digital trackers, can help students monitor their assigned stations and choices, ensuring everyone stays on track.
- **Use data strategically:** The success of this approach depends on accurately identifying must-do stations for each student. Use formative or summative assessment data to pinpoint specific learning needs and strengths. Assign one or two must-do stations to address these areas while reserving the may-do stations for student choice based on interests or preferences.

- **Clearly communicate the must-do stations:** Provide students with a clear understanding of their must-do stations by sharing a class list (e.g., on the board or through your LMS) or giving them individualized schedules, cards, or a personalized learning plan (as pictured in figure 11.1). This shifts the responsibility for documentation to students and eliminates confusion. Additionally, a posted rotation schedule with brief descriptions of each station helps students navigate their choices and plan their time effectively.

**Must-Do vs. May-Do Station Rotation**
Your Personalized Learning Plan

| Stations | Descriptions | | Your Notes & Reflections |
|---|---|---|---|
| | | | • Note which stations are your "must-do" learning activities.<br>• For your "may-do" stations, explain why you chose this station. |
| Teacher-Led Station | | | |
| | Rotation 1: [Skill/Concept/Focus] | | |
| | Rotation 2: [Skill/Concept/Focus] | | |
| | Rotation 3: [Skill/Concept/Focus] | | |
| | Rotation 4: [Skill/Concept/Focus] | | |
| Station 2 | [Insert Description] | | |
| Station 3 | [Insert Description] | | |
| Station 4 | [Insert Description] | | |
| Station 5 | [Insert Description] | | |
| Station 6 | [Insert Description] | | |

**Figure 11.1: Must-Do vs. May-Do Station Rotation Personalized Learning Plan**

When should a teacher consider using a must-do vs. may-do variation? The following situations lend themselves to this design:

- **Differentiation:** In a class with diverse skill levels, use assessment data to identify critical areas where individual

students need extra support. Must-do stations are tailored for skill reinforcement, while may-do stations offer extension activities, review games, and metacognitive skill-building activities.
- **Interest-based learning:** In a unit of study, set up must-do stations addressing core curriculum requirements and may-do stations that invite students to explore subtopics related to the subject, allowing students to choose based on their interests.
- **Preparation for an assessment:** To prepare for an upcoming test or assessment, must-do stations provide practice and support in areas where data shows students struggle. In contrast, may-do stations offer practice in areas where students feel they can benefit from additional practice and review.
- **Math skills reinforcement:** For math classes, must-do stations can focus on foundational math skills that need reinforcement, as identified by assessment data, while may-do stations could offer problem-solving activities, collaborative real-world math challenges, or math games that stimulate critical thinking and application.
- **Project-based learning (PBL):** In a PBL environment, must-do stations can be essential steps in the project process, such as research or prototype development, while may-do stations can offer optional skills workshops or resources for deepening project work, like using organizational project management tools or conducting interviews.

The must-do vs. may-do Station Rotation Model balances meeting students' individual needs and fostering their sense of autonomy. By tailoring required tasks to target specific learning goals and allowing students to choose how to spend the rest of their time, this approach supports personalized learning and student agency. It empowers students to take ownership of their learning while ensuring they engage in meaningful, data-informed activities that support their growth.

## Variation #3: Offering Optional Skill Stations

Optional skill stations offer a way to address variability in classrooms by providing targeted instruction and scaffolding for students who need it while allowing others to continue working independently.

How does this variation work? Optional skill stations are not embedded into a traditional Station Rotation Model but instead use the teacher-led station as a stand-alone, targeted support option. As the rest of the class engages in self-directed work—such as a writing assignment, research project, performance task, choice board, or playlist—use a solo, teacher-led station to provide structured small-group instruction focused on a specific skill that is proving challenging for some students.

For example, during a writing assignment, you may notice that several students struggle with crafting strong topic sentences, selecting strong textual evidence, or identifying passive versus active voice. You can offer an optional skills station where small groups of students can receive direct instruction, modeling, and guided practice to address specific challenges or learning gaps.

While the "optional" nature of the station allows most students to decide whether they need additional support, you can remove this component for certain students who require intervention. For example, you can require that students needing Tier 2 or Tier 3 intervention attend specific skill stations to address gaps in understanding. This flexibility ensures that students who need additional help do not fall behind.

By incorporating Tier 2 and Tier 3 interventions in the classroom, you can avoid pulling students out of the general education setting and instead provide the support they need within the context of their regular work. This integration fosters a more inclusive environment and ensures that intervention aligns closely with the learning tasks and goals of the broader class. This approach also maximizes your ability to meet a range of student needs, balancing personalized support for some with autonomy and choice for others.

When should a teacher consider offering optional skill stations?

They are particularly effective in classrooms where students are engaged in self-directed work. These stations provide targeted support when:

- **Students demonstrate skill gaps:** In this scenario, formative assessments or classroom observations reveal that specific students are struggling with particular skills, such as analyzing data, solving complex equations, or completing a writing assignment. The skill station allows these students to receive focused support while others continue working independently.
- **Tier 2 or Tier 3 support is needed:** For students requiring more intensive intervention, you can make the skill station mandatory, providing small-group instruction tailored to individuals' needs. Integrating these interventions into the classroom minimizes disruption and ensures alignment with the tasks the class is working on.
- **Students are working on complex, multi-step tasks:** Long-term assignments or projects often require the application of multiple skills. The skill station can address immediate challenges students face as they work, offering just-in-time support that keeps them progressing.

By using skill stations in these scenarios, teachers can create a classroom environment that is responsive to individual needs, providing the right level of support at the right time. This approach ensures that all students, regardless of their starting point, can make meaningful progress.

## Summary

The Station Rotation Model can be adapted to meet the diverse needs of learners while fostering student agency and personalized learning. By exploring creative variations, you can design dynamic learning environments that prioritize student autonomy, provide targeted support, and allow for meaningful choice. These approaches allow you to use data strategically to address skill gaps, provide Tier 2 and Tier 3 interventions, and offer timely, relevant instruction that aligns with students' ongoing work. Whether you're helping students self-pace through assignments or tailoring support to specific needs, these variations enhance the Station Rotation Model as a tool to engage students and promote equitable learning experiences.

## Reflect and Discuss

1. How might these variations of the Station Rotation Model shift the way students experience learning in your classroom? How do you think these variations might impact students' sense of ownership over their learning?

2. What logistical challenges do you anticipate, and how might you address them to ensure a smooth implementation? What systems can you put in place to ensure these potential challenges do not derail your lessons?

3. How could implementing a free-flow, student-paced rotation address the diverse pacing needs of your students? How might it impact student engagement? What strategies might you use to ensure all students remain productive and engaged while working at their own pace?

4. In what ways do these approaches align with your current goals for differentiation, personalized learning, and supporting diverse learners?
5. When would it be most beneficial for you to use the may-do vs. must-do design with your students? What types of data could you use to identify student needs? What strategy could you use to clearly communicate to each student which stations are must-dos? How can you have them track their may-do choices?
6. What skills or concepts have you observed your students struggling with that could be addressed through optional skill stations? How might you balance making the station optional while requiring intervention for students who need additional support?
7. How could integrating Tier 2 or Tier 3 interventions into your classroom through the must-do vs. may-do and optional skill stations make it easier to address the diverse needs of students in your class?

## Time to Apply: Design a Lesson

**Objective:** Select one of the three variations—free-flow, student-paced rotation; must-do vs. may-do; or optional skill stations—and design a lesson tailored to your students' needs. Follow the steps below to guide your planning process.

### Step 1: Identify Your Lesson Goals

Follow the advice below to set clear goals:

- Choose a topic, concept, or skill that your students are currently working on (e.g., writing, problem-solving, research, or project work).
- Define the primary learning objectives for the lesson.
- Consider which areas of differentiation or scaffolding might be necessary based on your students' needs.

## Step 2: Select a Station Rotation Variation

Choose one of the three variations to structure your lesson:

- **Free-flow, student-paced rotation:** Students self-pace through stations based on task completion.
- **Must-do vs. may-do stations:** Students are assigned required stations but have a choice about the other stations they go to.
- **Optional skill stations:** The teacher-led station provides targeted support related to a self-directed task.

## Step 3: Design Your Stations

Consider how you can optimize the stations of the variation structure you chose:

- Free-flow, student-paced rotations:
    - Create a series of learning activities that benefit from variable time on task.
    - Design a teacher-led station that is focused on feedback. What will you provide feedback on? What is the expectation for students once they receive the feedback?
- Must-do vs. may-do stations:
    - Use data to identify must-do stations for specific students and design may-do stations that provide meaningful choices.
    - Balance the stations with a mix of high-priority skill-building and engaging enrichment activities.
- Optional skill stations:
    - Identify a skill or concept that students may struggle with and design a teacher-led station offering direct instruction or guided practice.

○ Plan independent work that aligns with the skill being addressed.

## Step 4: Plan the Logistics

Consider details like the following:

- Articulate the "why" for your students, making it clear what the purpose of this design is for them.
- Determine how long each station will last or how many rotations will fit into your class period.
- Create a schedule, personalized learning plan, or visual tracker to help students navigate the stations.
- Consider how you will cue transitions and ensure smooth movement between tasks if needed.

## Step 5: Incorporate Reflection

Build time into the lesson for students to reflect on their experiences. For example, ask students:

- Which station was most helpful for your learning today?
- How did you use your time effectively?
- What skill or concept do you feel more confident about after this lesson?

## Step 6: Share Your Lesson Plan with a Colleague for Feedback

Make sure you leverage your peers to optimize your approach by taking the following steps:

- Share your completed lesson plan with a colleague or professional learning community for feedback.
- Discuss potential adjustments and reflect on how this variation could enhance learning in your classroom.

# Conclusion

Over the last twenty-five years, I have watched the spectrum of needs in classrooms widen. Teachers are working with increasingly diverse groups of students who enter classrooms with a range of skills, needs, languages, and lived experiences. Too often, this diversity is seen as a problem or a threat to the way we have always approached this work. That's a mistake. The beautiful diversity of students in our classrooms is not a problem; it is a reality we must design for to leverage the diversity as an asset to our learning community. When we recognize that reality, it becomes clear that the problem lies *not* in the differences among our students but in the rigid nature of the one-size-fits-all lesson.

Teachers need a more robust and flexible toolbox of instructional models to draw from as they design learning experiences for diverse populations of students. If the only instructional approach they know how to use is the whole-group, teacher-led, teacher-paced lesson, teachers will continue to feel frustrated while falling short of meeting many of their students' needs. At the same time, many students will continue to spend their days in classrooms that are rigid, uninspiring, and poorly equipped to meet their unique needs.

To design more accessible, inclusive, and equitable learning experiences, teachers need instructional models that free them to meet the needs of individual students and small groups. The Station Rotation Model is one instructional design teachers can add to their toolbox to get closer to meeting the needs of all students in their classes, all while elevating the effectiveness of Tier 1 instruction and making time for Tier 2 and Tier 3 interventions. The Station Rotation Model provides an avenue for designing lessons that give students more opportunities to control the pace at which they acquire new information, process and make meaning, and apply their learning, both on their own and in collaboration with their peers. Moreover, educators can leverage this model to create flexible pathways that allow all learners to progress with the necessary support toward clear, standards-aligned learning goals.

However, to accomplish the goal of designing equitable learning experiences, teachers don't just need new models; they also need the confidence to embrace change, an understanding of how to design learning with inclusive instructional strategies, and the tools to design for the diversity present in every classroom. This work demands not just a shift in practice but also a shift in mindset—away from control and conformity and toward creativity, collaboration, and flexibility.

Teachers are the lead learners in a classroom, and in a world that is evolving at an unprecedented pace, this role has never been more important. The world beyond our classrooms is changing rapidly—technological advancements, shifting industries, and global challenges require individuals who can think critically, adapt, collaborate, and contribute meaningfully to society. If we hope to send our students into this dynamic landscape prepared to thrive, we must model the very skills and mindsets we wish to cultivate in them.

Embracing new approaches to teaching may feel daunting, but it is also an opportunity to grow, experiment, and evolve alongside our students. By trying new instructional strategies, inviting student feedback, and demonstrating resilience in the face of challenges, we create classrooms where curiosity, risk-taking, and perseverance are celebrated. These are the environments where students feel empowered to explore their potential and build the skills they will need to navigate and shape the future.

Remember, transformative change does not require overhauling everything at once. Sustainable progress is built on small, intentional steps. Start by implementing just one strategy from this book. Perhaps you begin with a simple rotation using familiar activities to help students adjust to a new way of learning. From there, experiment with differentiating your teacher-led station, leveraging feedback to refine your practice. Every small adjustment is a step toward a more inclusive, equitable, and student-centered classroom.

As teachers, our willingness to learn, adapt, and grow sends a powerful message to our students: Learning is a lifelong journey. Together, we can reimagine education, one step at a time, creating classrooms that not only meet the needs of every student but inspire them to shape the world beyond our walls.

# References

### Introduction
1. Karla Wang, "Differentiation: Achieving Success in a Mixed-Ability Classroom," *The Science of Learning Blog*, July 11, 2019, https://www.scilearn.com/differentiation-achieving-success-mixed-ability-classroom.
2. Katie Novak and Catlin R. Tucker, *UDL and Blended Learning: Thriving in Flexible Learning Landscapes* (IMPress, 2021), 6–8.
3. Eleanor Fulbeck et al., *Personalizing Student Learning with Station Rotation: A Descriptive Study*, American Institutes for Research, July 2020, https://www.air.org/sites/default/files/Station-Rotation-Research-Brief-Final-July-2020.pdf.

### Chapter 1
1. CAST, *UDL Guidelines* (version 3.0), 2024, https://udlguidelines.cast.org.

### Chapter 2
1. E. L. Deci and R. M. Ryan, *Intrinsic Motivation and Self-Determination in Human Behavior* (Springer Science & Business Media, 2013).
2. "Supporting Students' Self-Regulated and Self-Directed Learning in the Remote Environment," University of Guelph's Office of Teaching and Learning, https://otl.uoguelph.ca/teaching-remotely/remote-teaching-strategies/supporting-students%E2%80%99-self-regulated-and-self-directed.
3. Pooja K. Agarwal and Patrice M. Bain, *Powerful Teaching: Unleash the Science of Learning* (Jossey-Bass, 2019).

### Chapter 3
1. Francesca Paris and Sarah Mervosh, "Why School Absences Have 'Exploded' Almost Everywhere," *New York Times*, March 29, 2024, https://www.nytimes.com/interactive/2024/03/29/us/chronic-absences.html.
2. Carol Ann Tomlinson, *How to Differentiate Instruction in Academically Diverse Classrooms*, 3rd ed. (ASCD, 2024).
3. "Definition of MTSS," California Department of Education, July 24, 2024, https://www.cde.ca.gov/ci/cr/ri/mtsscomprti2.asp.
4. Sarah W. Siegal et al., *Aligning Practice with Research: Using Small Groups to Differentiate Instruction*, Scholastic Research & Validation (Scholastic, 2024).
5. Saiying Steenbergen-Hu et al., "What One Hundred Years of Research Says About the Effects of Ability Grouping and Acceleration on K–12 Students' Academic Achievement: Findings of Two Second-Order Meta-Analyses," *Review of Educational Research* 86, no. 4 (2016): 849–899.
6. Noelle Gutierrez and Catlin Tucker, "Creating Inclusive Classrooms with Co-Teaching and the Station Rotation," Dr. Catlin Tucker, August 23, 2024, https://catlintucker.com/2024/08/creating-inclusive-classrooms-with-co-teaching.

## Chapter 6

1. Alex Kostogriz and Nikolay Veresov, "The Zone of Proximal Development and Diversity," Oxford Research Encyclopedia of Education, June 28, 2021, https://doi.org/10.1093/acrefore/9780190264093.013.1542.
2. Carol Ann Tomlinson, "What Is Differentiated Instruction and Why Differentiate?," *Differentiated Instruction: An Introduction*, Module 1, ASCD Professional Development Online (ASCD, 2010), 1, https://pdo.ascd.org/LMSCourses/PD11OC115M/media/DI-Intro_M1_Reading_What_Is_DI.pdf.
3. Carol Ann Tomlinson, *The Differentiated Classroom: Responding to the Needs of All Learners*, 2nd ed. (ASCD, 2014).
4. Grant Wiggins, "Seven Keys to Effective Feedback," ASCD, September 1, 2012, https://ascd.org/el/articles/seven-keys-to-effective-feedback.
5. Valerie J. Shute, "Focus on Formative Feedback," *Review of Educational Research* 78, no. 1 (2008): 153–189.

## Chapter 7

1. Catlin Tucker, host, *The Balance*, podcast, episode 23, "Reclaiming Personalized Learning with Paul France," January 9, 2021, https://podcasts.apple.com/es/podcast/reclaiming-personalized-learning-with-paul-france/id1485751335?i=1000534012808&l=ca.
2. Bernard Marr, "The Top 10 Most In-Demand Skills for the Next 10 Years," *Forbes*, August 22, 2022, www.forbes.com/sites/bernardmarr/2022/08/22/the-top-10-most-in-demand-skills-for-the-next-10-years.
3. Jenny Anderson and Rebecca Winthrop, *The Disengaged Teen: Helping Kids Learn Better, Feel Better, and Live Better* (Crown, 2025).
4. Ruben R. Puentedura, "SAMR: Moving from Enhancement to Transformation," *Ruben R. Puentedura's Weblog*, 2014, http://www.hippasus.com/rrpweblog/archives/2013/05/29/SAMREnhancementToTransformation.pdf.

## Chapter 8

1. Richard M. Ryan and Edward L. Deci, *Self-Determination Theory: Basic Psychological Needs in Motivation, Development, and Wellness* (Guilford Publications, 2017).
2. Michael Tomasello, "An Agency-Based Model of Executive and Metacognitive Regulation," *Frontiers in Developmental Psychology* 15 vol. 2 (March 7, 2024): Article 1367381, https://doi.org/10.3389/fdpys.2024.1367381.
3. Erika A. Patall et al., "The Effects of Choice on Intrinsic Motivation and Related Outcomes: A Meta-Analysis of Research Findings," *Psychological Bulletin* 134, no. 2 (2008): 270–300.
4. Tania Zittoun and Svend Brinkmann, "Learning as Meaning Making," in *Encyclopedia of the Sciences of Learning*, ed. Norbert M. Seel (Springer, 2012), https://doi.org/10.1007/978-1-4419-1428-6_1851.
5. David Ritchie and Belinda D. Karge, "Making Information Memorable: Enhanced Knowledge Retention and Recall Through the Elaboration Process," *Preventing School Failure: Alternative Education for Children and Youth* 41, no. 1 (2010): 28–33.
6. Claire E. Weinstein et al., "Self-Regulation and Learning Strategies," *New Directions for Teaching and Learning* 2011, no. 126 (2011): 45–53, https://doi.org/10.1002/tl.443.

# References

7. Wolfgang Schneider, "The Development of Metacognitive Knowledge in Children and Adolescents: Major Trends and Implications for Education," *Mind, Brain, and Education* 2, no. 3 (2008): 114–121, https://doi.org/10.1111/j.1751-228X.2008.00041.x.
8. John Hattie, "The Applicability of Visible Learning to Higher Education," *Scholarship of Teaching and Learning in Psychology* 1 (1) (2015): 79–91, https://doi.org/10.1037/stl0000021.
9. Jonathan Perry et al., "Metacognition in Schools: What Does the Literature Suggest About the Effectiveness of Teaching Metacognition in Schools?," *Educational Review* 71 (4) (2018): 483–500, https://doi.org/10.1080/00131911.2018.1441127.
10. "Thinking Routine Toolbox," Project Zero, Harvard Graduate School of Education, https://pz.harvard.edu/thinking-routines.

## Chapter 9

1. "Thinking Routine Toolbox," Project Zero, Harvard Graduate School of Education, https://pz.harvard.edu/thinking-routines.
2. Noelle Gutierrez, "How to Incorporate a Relaxation Station to Prioritize Student Well-Being," Dr. Catlin Tucker, October 28, 2024, https://catlintucker.com/2024/10/relaxation-station.
3. Simon Sinek, *Start with Why: How Great Leaders Inspire Everyone to Take Action* (Penguin, 2009), 19.
4. Gretchen Brion-Meisels, "Step 3: Norm-Setting to Build Brave Spaces," Instructional Moves, Educating for Equity and Inclusion, Harvard Graduate School of Education, https://instructionalmoves.gse.harvard.edu/inclusivity-and-belonging/step-3-norm-setting-to-build-brave-spaces.
5. "Building Inclusive Classrooms," Center for Teaching Innovation, Cornell University, 2024, https://teaching.cornell.edu/teaching-resources/building-inclusive-classrooms.

## Chapter 10

1. Sarah W. Siegal, Colby Hall, and Michael P. Mesa, *Aligning Practice with Research: Using Small Groups to Differentiate Instruction* (New York: Scholastic, 2024).
2. Vincent J. Granito and Mary E. Santana, "Psychology of Learning Spaces: Impact on Teaching and Learning," *Journal of Learning Spaces* 5, no. 1 (2016): 1–8.
3. Ozan Kepez and Selen Üst, "Furniture Configurations in an Active Learning Classroom Make Further Differences in Student Outcomes," *Archnet-IJAR: International Journal of Architectural Research* 18, no. 1 (2024): 121–141.
4. Julia D. Stanton et al., "Fostering Metacognition to Support Student Learning and Performance," *CBE—Life Sciences Education* 20, no. 2 (2021): fe3, https://doi.org/10.1187/cbe.20-12-0289.

# Acknowledgments

Cheyenne and Maddox: You fill my life with light and purpose. You inspire me daily to continue this work. I love you to the moon and back.

Chris: Your love and support are gifts. You help me weather life's stressful moments. Thank you for lightening my load when life gets busy and for reminding me to slow down and breathe. I appreciate you more than you'll ever know.

George and Paige: Thank you for your continued support of my work and your willingness to share my ideas with educators. Your belief in this work means the world to me.

To the educators I've had the privilege of working with: Thank you for trusting me, welcoming me into your classrooms, and embracing the challenge of reimagining teaching and learning. Your passion, creativity, and courage continue to fuel my commitment to this work.

# About Catlin R. Tucker

Dr. Catlin Tucker is a bestselling author, international trainer, and keynote speaker. She was named Teacher of the Year in 2010 in Sonoma County, where she taught for sixteen years. Catlin earned her BA in English literature from the University of California at Los Angeles, then earned her English teaching credential and master's in education from the University of California at Santa Barbara. In 2020, she earned her doctorate in learning technologies from Pepperdine University.

Catlin designs and facilitates professional learning experiences that empower leaders and teachers to cultivate the mindset, skill set, and tool set needed to design equitable, student-centered learning environments. She focuses on data-informed design, differentiation, and personalized learning to meet the diverse needs of all students. By leveraging technology strategically, Catlin helps educators shift from being the sole source of knowledge to facilitators who actively engage students as agents in their own learning. She also collaborates with leadership teams and instructional coaches to create professional learning infrastructures that embed growth and innovation into the fabric of school communities, ensuring sustainable and meaningful change.

In addition to her work in K–12 education, Catlin is a professor in the Master of Arts in Teaching program at Pepperdine University, where she supports teacher candidates in developing their instructional methods and practices.

Catlin has written a series of bestselling books, including *Elevating Educational Design with AI*, *The Shift to Student-Led*, *The Complete Guide to Blended Learning*, *UDL and Blended Learning*, and *Balance with Blended Learning*. She hosts *The Balance* podcast and is active on X @Catlin_Tucker and Instagram @CatlinTucker. You can learn more about her work at CatlinTucker.com.

# More from IMPRESS

ImpressBooks.org

*Empower: What Happens When Students Own Their Learning* by A.J. Juliani and John Spencer

*Learner-Centered Innovation: Spark Curiosity, Ignite Passion, and Unleash Genius* by Katie Martin

*Unleash Talent: Bringing Out the Best in Yourself and the Learners You Serve* by Kara Knollmeyer

*Reclaiming Our Calling: Hold On to the Heart, Mind, and Hope of Education* by Brad Gustafson

*Take the L.E.A.P.: Ignite a Culture of Innovation* by Elisabeth Bostwick

*Drawn to Teach: An Illustrated Guide to Transforming Your Teaching* written by Josh Stumpenhorst and illustrated by Trevor Guthke

*Math Recess: Playful Learning in an Age of Disruption* by Sunil Singh and Dr. Christopher Brownell

*Innovate inside the Box: Empowering Learners Through UDL and Innovator's Mindset* by George Couros and Katie Novak

*Personal & Authentic: Designing Learning Experiences That Last a Lifetime* by Thomas C. Murray

*Learner-Centered Leadership: A Blueprint for Transformational Change in Learning Communities* by Devin Vodicka

*Kids These Days: A Game Plan for (Re)Connecting with Those We Teach, Lead, & Love* by Dr. Jody Carrington

*UDL and Blended Learning: Thriving in Flexible Learning Landscapes* by Katie Novak and Catlin Tucker

*Teachers These Days: Stories & Strategies for Reconnection* by Dr. Jody Carrington and Laurie McIntosh

*Because of a Teacher: Stories of the Past to Inspire the Future of Education* written and curated by George Couros

*Because of a Teacher, Volume 2: Stories from the First Years of Teaching* written and curated by George Couros

*Evolving Education: Shifting to a Learner-Centered Paradigm* by Katie Martin

*Adaptable: How to Create an Adaptable Curriculum and Flexible Learning Experiences That Work in Any Environment* by A.J. Juliani

*Lead from Where You Are: Building Intention, Connection, and Direction in Our Schools* by Joe Sanfelippo

*The Shift to Student-Led: Reimagining Classroom Workflows with UDL and Blended Learning* by Catlin R. Tucker & Katie Novak

*The Design Thinking Classroom: Using Design Thinking to Reimagine the Role and Practice of Educators* by David Jakes

*Shift Writing into the Classroom with UDL and Blended Learning* by Catlin R. Tucker and Katie Novak

*Teach Happy: Small Steps to Big Joy* by Kim Strobel

*What Makes a Great Principal* by George Couros and Allyson Apsey

*Hopes for School: A Student's Experience and Ideas for Educational Transformation* by Karen Phan & Jennifer Casa-Todd

www.ingramcontent.com/pod-product-compliance
Lightning Source LLC
Chambersburg PA
CBHW050518170426
43201CB00013B/2006